How to make a living as an artist.

▼

Colin Ruffell

www.crabfish.com

for my wife and partner

Fran Slade

ACKNOWLEDGEMENTS

Special thanks to the contributors to this book, and to the others who inspired me knowingly or unknowingly. They include in alphabetical order,

Natasha Barnes, Larry Berman, Harry Bilson, Willie Crawford, Jim Edwards, Andy Hoogenboom, Brooks Jensen, Harald Johnson, John Kehoe, Man Creates Art Creates Man, New York Society of Etchers, Brett Raven, Mike Sims and the staff at The Fine Art Trade Guild, Alice Tickner, Michael Tickner.

Very special thanks to David Longman who suggested many improvements, which have been gratefully received and eagerly adopted.

Published by www.howtobeanartist.com

First Published August 2004 [e-book]

First printed edition May 2005

[special illustrated signed and numbered edition of 100]

CONTENTS

INTRODUCTION

The book is aimed at the many wannabe artists who would like to know how to make a full time living as a real artist.

The big questions are

- How to sell your art?
- How to make money from art?
- How to survive as an artist?
- How to succeed as an artist?
- How to avoid the pitfalls?
- How to overcome the mind blocks?

This e-book is not called 'How to paint pictures', and so it is not about painting techniques. Maybe that book will come later.

This book is about how YOU can be a real full time professional artist.

First things first. You should forget the various pessimistic myths about the art business that say that making a living doing your art is impossible.

It is certainly possible to be a successful full time artist.

You do not have to be a genius either. Neither do you need to be particularly lucky, well connected, or rich. You can do it even if you are poor, moderately talented, with no connections, and without needing buckets of good luck. I know because I have been doing it for forty years. And although I went to two different art colleges, you don't actually need to have any training at all.

A good way to start believing this, and believing in yourself as an artist, is to realise that you have the colossal advantage of having two brains. You are in effect a twin. You have a left-brain and you have a right brain. Just like everybody else that lives on this planet.

The difference between being an artist and being a non-artist is that most non-artists gradually lose much of the intuitive and creative power of the right brain by the time they are adult.

You want to be an artist and so it is very likely that you will have retained use of the right side of your brain. You probably enjoy creating your art, and you do not want to witness the eventual death of your creative side. You do not want your twin to die.

Maybe you dislike or even dread the boring experience that a life of dry responsible left-brain activity alone involves. But the stereotypical alternative, namely of being an eccentric bohemian artist, using only irresponsible right brain power, and living in poverty, is not acceptable to you either.

This book can show you how to combine the power of both brains to enrich your life, survive, and succeed, as an artist, and be a responsible and respected member of society.

The crucial difference between a successful artist, and a failure, is that **<u>a successful artist uses both brains</u>**. The left-brain does all the logical business stuff, and the right brain does all the creative stuff.

It is like having two super computers linked by a network. Both computers receive the same input signals coming through your senses, hearing, touch, smell, taste and sight. The left uses the information in one way, while the right uses it another way. You, and your twin, are an artist.

OK, so the twin brain idea is not strictly accurate in neuro-biological terms. It is an analogy. It is 'as if' we successful artists have two brains.

In this book you will find twelve golden rules, and four nasty shocks. You will be shown eight strategies for survival. And you will be told about a number of other advantages and benefits. For instance, the high social status of artists despite the incredibly inexpensive set up costs plus huge profit margins for making art. And about the fact that an artist can be fast and flexible as a small one-person business, and survive and prosper in the huge art industry that relies on a steady stream of art from people like you and me.

You will be shown how to achieve the practical competence, and inner confidence, that are necessary to survive and succeed on your path to becoming a full time professional artist.

CHAPTER ONE: It's a set up

In which we discuss setting up

your studio, your office, your workshop,

your exhibition system, your transport.

And where we give you some good news.

And your first three golden rules.

Setting up your studio.

****** GOOD NEWS ...... NUMBER ONE *******

Here is some good news. **You will need a minimum of capital to start.**

You could have as little as one piece of paper, and a pencil, and draw your first ever picture today, sell it this evening, and tomorrow go buy a big box of paints and a load of brushes.

Not many businesses have start up opportunities like that!

But I don't expect that you are starting absolutely from scratch.

I fact, you have probably already started, so lets look at what you have got.

- Have you a room or space of your own?
- Have you a few ordinary paints and paper or canvas?

If yes then you probably already have a few finished paintings.

So you are already on the way. You do not need any more to start!

I have known artists who were making a good living who used to paint in their kitchen, with the canvas propped up on an upside down chair on the kitchen table, using student quality paints onto hardboard [Masonite] panels. Alfred Wallace the Cornish artist painted onto cardboard torn from cardboard boxes.

What I am saying is that you really don't need much to start.

******* GOOD NEWS ...... NUMBER TWO ********

Another big, big benefit of this art business, is that as sales and money come in **you will have gross profit margins that would make any other business owner weep with envy.**

Gross profit margins are the difference between the cost of making the item for sale and the selling price. Here is a simple rule of thumb. On average it costs about one tenth of the selling price to make the art object.

So if you want to sell a picture for one thousand dollars/pounds/euros you would expect to spend about one hundred on paint, paper or canvas, and frame. One hundred turns into one thousand.

That is a one thousand percent mark-up.

And that is why it is unusually simple and inexpensive to start.

And that is why you can make a profit from this business.

Compare an artist's set up costs with almost anybody else and we artists have a massive advantage. No factories to buy, no staff to hire, no leases, licenses, and landlords to negotiate, no costly machinery, no fleets of trucks, no stock of raw materials. And even better, artists have a huge gross profit margin of a thousand percent.

Now does that make you feel a bit better? It should.

But it doesn't mean that you can book a holiday in the sun straight away. You will need to make profits from next to nothing so that you can grow as an artist.

It would be very good to realise from the start that you should invest your profits back into your art-business, whenever you can, because you are investing in your-self and your future. You are worth investing in, and worth believing in.

You will soon find that you will want more space, more equipment, more expensive and better quality paints and canvas. You will want to have big studio easels, special lights, pure sable brushes, etc..

You might have to wait until the artist/ business you are in has a bit of spare profit. But then it should be your intention to re-invest a good chunk of the profit back into your new business, the business of being an artist.

This book is laced with   **GOLDEN RULES** ...... so here is the first;

GOLDEN RULE No 1; INVEST, AND BELIEVE, IN YOURSELF.

You are the prime asset of your new business. Any successful business person will tell you that you have got to nurture and protect your prime asset. As any gardener will tell you, you should water and feed your precious plants to get the best from your garden.

The same goes in your new art business. You must nurture and invest in yourself at every opportunity. You are the treasure store in your palace; you are the goose that will lay the golden eggs.

You will be interested to know what you will eventually need to be able to run yourself as a professional artist.

Here is my own studio inventory as an example.

Studio kit

> 2 studio easels.
>
> Work bench
>
> Lights
>
> Lots of paint, medium and pigment.
>
> Varnish, fixative spray,
>
> Set of drawers filled with other stuff, polish, ink, wax, pens, toothbrushes, rulers, etc.. [junk mostly]
>
> Brushes, rollers, painting knives etc.
>
> Paper, canvas, panels.

Setting up your office/work-station.

Now we come to the next stage of this overview of your business position. You will have to organise part of your studio to take care of the flip side of the artist business coin.

You must also sell your art.

Whereas the cost of making art can be quite small, the total cost of selling can be much higher.

Remember here we just talk about your set up procedure and costs.

You will need to keep good office records, the cost of a computer and printer and phone line, broadband internet connection, etc must be your major priority. This where a good artist can fail just as he/she is getting started. Please get yourself a desk space and shelving for record keeping. Please, please, please, from day one, keep records, keep accounts, and make notes of your business ideas and details, as well as your artistic creation.

Get into the habit of noting names and addresses, phone numbers and email and websites of everyone that you come into contact with in your new business. Think of the office part of the art business as a place you love to be in as much as the studio. You will probably spend as much time at your desk as you do at your easel when you are successful and pulling in the big money. So enjoy it. Enjoy being an artist/business and do it well.

If you really hate this part of the new lifestyle then you must get a partner to do it. You will not make it past the first stages without an organised admin/sales capability. Either tackle the task yourself or get it organised so that someone else does it. It has to be done well!

GOLDEN RULE No 2: KEEP RECORDS

Record keeping seems like a boring chore, but it is not. You will soon make use of your records. You will find that you examine the records that you keep over and over again. The records that you start keeping now will show you how well you are doing, or where you are going wrong. You shouldn't have to guess, or rack your brains remembering, when you want to find out who it was, or when, or how much, or why something happened.

Your office could be the most expensive part of setting up as an artist.

Example;

Here is my own office inventory.

Office kit

> 1 120 gig computer with 200 gig slave drive
>
> 1 Laptop computer plus 120 gig external memory drive
>
> 1 Wacom Cintique tablet
>
> 1 big desk and shelving space
>
> 1 x Epson 9600 printer

1 x Fax machine

1 x Epson R800 desktop printer

2 plan chests, 2 filing cabinets

1 Fuji Finepix 7000 digital camera

1 Canon digital camera 4 megapixel.

1 x A4 scanner

******* GOOD NEWS ......NUMBER THREE ********

Computers will help you enormously.

You would be mad to get into the art business without using the powerful tools available in a computerised office workstation.

You could do this without a computer of course. I didn't have a computer when I started because they were not around then. Oh the good old days with double entry book keeping and card indexes. Hah! Give me the joy of computerisation any day.

This is not the time to go deeply into the PC or Mac debate. But if you have arrived on this planet from outer space and have not already got a computer, you will notice that there are two main contenders for your attention. The world's favourite platform is the PC running Windows. But many artists and designers opt for the Mac. I chose a PC platform many years ago when I first got a computer and I have stuck to it since. They say that 95% of home computers run on this system

But my daughter went to Art College and learnt on a Mac, so she has opted for that now that she has set up as a professional artist/designer.

She swears that it is more intuitive and friendlier than a PC.

In actual fact the systems are becoming more and more interchangeable, so your choice of platform will not be quite as crucial in the future.

Setting up your workshop.

OK, so back to the studio. It is my experience that the studio has two departments.

- A painting section where you paint, which was mentioned earlier,

- and your workshop section where you prepare canvases, make frames etc..

This is where you must think about presentation, framing and displaying.

You will be paid back over and over again if you frame your work well. That does not mean that your art has to be framed expensively. You can make your own frames with a simple mitre saw and timber from your local timber merchant. Do it as well as you can. Don't skimp on the frame either. A big hand finished frame can make a small picture have much more value than the same picture in a miserly thin frame done in cheap unpainted do-it-yourself picture edging. Have a look at art in exhibitions and see what the opposition is doing. If you cannot frame it yourself then get someone to help you. Your aim is to have a high-quality good-looking piece of art. You will be able to charge much more for the piece if it is well presented.

GOLDEN RULE No 3: AIM FOR QUALITY.

Quality is a thing. There is a wonderful book about this. In my local art college library I found a whole shelf with many copies of the book, 'Zen and the Art of Motorcycle Maintenance' by Robert Pirsig. The gurus at the art college realize that the quest for quality is an absolute must for the art student. Robert Pirsig's book tells it all. If you haven't read it yet, please do so soon.

The workshop need only be a space in your garage, or a garden shed. It will be where you make sawdust, and other debris from mucky tasks, so it should be separate from your clean studio. If you have not got the space at the beginning try to work towards it as soon as possible.

It has taken me many years but now I possess the following equipment;

Workshop kit.

1 foot operated mitre guillotine

1 foot operated mitre underpinner

1 4ft mount/matt cutter

1 big box of tools including, power drills, power planes, bradawls, canvas stretchers, staple gun, pin hammer, gentleman's saw, mitre vice, power screwdriver, power sander, etc..

Setting up exhibition stuff.

You might not need to get into much exhibition expense in the very early stages of your new career. But when you do you will probably look for, lights, browsers, trolley, portfolios, business brochures, order pads, catalogues, and display easels.

My own exhibition inventory consists of;

Exhibition kit

Laptop computer, [already mentioned].

Exhibition lights

Display counter.

Large print browser and 30 sleeves.

Medium print browser.

3 small print browsers.

1 Card spinner/card rack.

Plus lots of brochures, and assorted paperwork.

Setting up your transport.

You will need a big car or van with a lot of space to carry pictures and frames and everything else a professional artist possesses. I know that you could start without one. I did. But you will be showing how serious you take your new professional art business career if you sell your two seater sports model and get a Transit van or Volvo estate. [I still use a Volvo estate and it serves me well!]

In the USA you can see professional artists with sign written panel vans whenever you go to an art fair. I have known artist exhibitors who have a caravan or motor home that serves as a big delivery van, plus saves on hotel expenses when exhibiting away from home.

Total cost to set up

It has taken me many years to get my stuff together. You don't need all this from day one!

My total kit would cost about £15K [$27000] to buy or replace today. A small investment when you consider my turnover.

But I started with almost nothing, and so can you.

****** GOOD NEWS ......NUMBER FOUR ********

The very nature of being an artist is that you are a small business, in fact a very small business. Probably the best example possible of a one-man band. And the really good thing about being small is that you are

- **fast**
- **flexible**
- **expert**

You can run rings around most opposition because you can react very swiftly to opportunities, you can change course on a dime, and you are the world's number one expert on you and your work.

Chapter One....Conclusion.

You can start with nothing! You will gradually add equipment paid for by your earnings.

Or you can jump in with some capital and give yourself a head start.

You have been given four pieces of very good news:

- start up capital is zero
- profit margins are enormous
- computers make the job easy
- small is beautiful and quick

And so far you have three golden rules.

GOLDEN RULE No 1:   **INVEST AND BELIEVE IN YOURSELF.**

GOLDEN RULE No 2:   **KEEP RECORDS.**

GOLDEN RULE No 3:   **AIM FOR QUALITY.**

GOLDEN RULE No 4:   **?.**

GOLDEN RULE No 5:   **?**

GOLDEN RULE No 6:   **?.**

GOLDEN RULE No 7:   **?**

GOLDEN RULE No 8:   **?**

GOLDEN RULE No 9:   **?**

GOLDEN RULE No 10:   **?**

GOLDEN RULE No 11:   **?**

GOLDEN RULE No 12:   **?**

CHAPTER TWO: Now you are in business

In which we discuss the business of being an artist,

your business strategy,

keeping records,

understanding and controlling costs,

getting professional help and advice,

legal issues,

tax [urgh!],

and copyright

And we introduce another two golden rules

Organising your business strategy,

This is just as important as chapter one. No in fact I reckon that it might be more important. For many wannabe artists the dream is to paint pictures full time. But reality will mean that you will have to sell as well.

Selling means that you will have to be organised.

Being organised means that you must recognise that you are a one-man/woman business now.

Being a business means that you will have to use the other side of your brain as well.

But hey, the other side of your brain can be just as much fun to use as the creative artistic side if you are doing it for yourself.

[There is a common misunderstanding that the left-brain is totally logical and the right-brain is spiritual and artistic. In fact it is not that simple. However, the left-brain is usually language led and thus more socially conditioned. Meanwhile the right-brain can operate without formal language and can be more intuitive. Most people use the left brain more and more as they get older and develop formal language skills, whilst the intuitive right-brain loses influence. As a small-business person you will continue to use the left hemisphere. As an artist you will enjoy using the right hemisphere. You will use both brains jointly.]

******* GOOD NEWS .... NUMBER FIVE ********

It is just as much fun being an artist business person, as it is being an artist creator person.

This is because the rewards of being successful are very good for your self-esteem and it feels wonderful when you sell well. You will find that you will develop new relationships with your customer/collectors dealers and exhibitors. These relationships are a real bonus to the artist's lifestyle. There are new friends and business partners out there who want you to be a new successful artist. Your business strategy needs to recognise the importance of finding them.

You might have read that professional artists should expect to spend 50% of their working week selling and administrating.

I know that it can be even more as you get more successful. So you might as well be good at it, and enjoy the office/administration side of your new lifestyle. It can be fun because you are doing it for yourself, and you can do it your own way.

So, let us examine the basics.

- You will make art.
- You will present your art to possible buyers.
- You will sell the art to buyers.
- You will do this soon enough and often enough so that you will be able to continue to greater rewards.

This book does not need to tell you how to create the actual art because there are zillions of ways to do that successfully.

But it will tell you how to present your art, how to sell your art and how to do it enough.

GOLDEN RULE No 4: BE BUSINESSLIKE.

The secret is to recognise that basic business strategy is the same for all businesses. Being an artist is no different. The laws of physics, economics, and success are the same for us all.

You will have to keep records.
- Records of financial transactions...ALL financial transactions.
- Records of inquiries, customers and potential leads.

- Records of your creations.

So you need to have the tools to keep these records. Nowadays the average home computer is powerful enough to do this. So get a simple accounts package, get a simple word processor, get a simple database, get an image-processing package, and learn how to use them.

Your financial records.

There is just no choice here. You have got to keep good financial records.

But you probably don't know anything about 'double entry ledgers' or the difference between input and output.

Fear not, it is not rocket science.

You will be able to get someone else to do the tricky stuff.

You will be quite capable of doing the straightforward simple stuff.

What you must do is keep records.

You need a book [ledger] to record your spending with a column each showing

1.   date that you spent the money

2.   item details [example; paint or train fare]

3.   amount in full

4.   how paid [example cash, cheque, card]

And you need another book showing income and sales with columns for

1. date

2. item

3. amount

4. how paid

Do this from today!

Later you will be able to move up a notch with help from a bookkeeper accountant or financial advisor.

Spike.

Always ask for receipts. Use cash as little as possible because it is harder to keep track of your spending.

First thing, buy a spike. A spike is one of those pointy metal things on a wooden base that sits on your desk and you spear all your receipts on it daily. Yes daily. At the end of the month sort them out into business expenses and personal pleasure expenses.

Overheads.

Work out your spending needs. Your rent or mortgage costs, your maintenance costs, heating lighting and other basic costs that cannot be avoided. Work out how much you need for food and clothing.

These are your overheads.

Cash flow forecast.

Make a yearly total of your overheads, divide by twelve and make simple monthly cash flow forecast chart to show these outgoings. Adjust to show payments that are made annually or quarterly.

Now you can see that you will need an income that will cover those overhead outgoings, plus the cost of getting that income.

Incurred costs.

The other kind of costs is the incurred costs that go up as you sell your art. They include your materials, your selling costs and other costs.

I have already said that your easy rule of thumb will be that each pound/euro/dollar coming in will have cost you one-tenth in material costs.

So what other costs do you have?

You have selling costs, you have research and development costs, you have travel costs, you have wages and commissions, you have taxes, and you have wastage and mistakes to allow for.

You will have to make estimates in order that you can now work out what your total income needs to be.

Then you can put them all into a standard cash flow forecast.

It is about time that you had another piece of good news

******* GOOD NEWS .... NUMBER SIX *******

There is plenty of free advice to be had for the asking

Professional advice

It would be a good idea if you go to your bank, or local chamber of commerce, and ask for their help in setting yourself up as a small business. They have a ready supply of cash flow forecast forms and plenty of advice ready for you. They will treat you just as any other small business and look at you to see whether you have a simple business plan and potential.

Be warned! They will **not** realise that you are an artist, and therefore a very special person, who deserves to have a free supply of money to enable the creative process. Neither will anybody else unless you are very lucky indeed. Let us assume that you are not very lucky!

So here are your priorities:

- keep records,
- see yourself as a small business,
- get as much help and advice as you can,
- use established small business techniques to survive.

Do these things even if you do not need the money, maybe you are wealthy, living on savings or a pension, or relying on a spouse or relative for your income. The discipline will do you some good, and the nurturing of the other side of your brain will make you a better artist. Maybe it is blood flow or neural expansion or something.

GOLDEN RULE No 5: SEEK, AND LISTEN TO, EXPERT ADVICE.

It can be humiliating for some people to ask for advice or help. How silly! The people who give advice do so willingly, and usually enjoy giving. There is a wealth of free advice available. Just ask!

Why reinvent the wheel?

Your database of customers, enquiries and leads.

I have come across many artists who gave up, or lived a life of poverty, because they failed to realise that 'keeping good customer records is very important'. Here is one reason why.

80/20 split.

In business practice there is a simple rule, look for the 80/20 split.

Eighty percent of your income comes from twenty percent of your effort.

That also means that only 20% of your income comes from 80% of your effort. Yikes!

You have got to constantly look for new ways of finding the 80/20 split. It changes as other things change.

Example.

For instance, you will probably find that you will sell far more pictures to people who already have one of your pictures than to new customers. It took me some time to notice this, but it is now blindingly obvious ... I sell 80% of my work to people who already own something else by me, and 20% to new customers.

Nowadays my established dealers buy most of my work. Previously the 80% were the people who I went to see in their homes, or came to see me in mine.

When I found that 80% came from established customers I also found to my horror that 80% of my selling effort was going into trying to find, and sell to, new customers. So I switched my attention and started to concentrate on old customers, and my sales went up.

You will need to keep good records in order to identify your own 80/20 split. When you do find the significant split you can focus on the areas of your business that actually work for you.

There is more about this later in the book.

Your record of your creations.

Your everyday PC will probably come with a Microsoft package that includes Access and Excel. These are ideal programmes to keep the kind of records that you should try to keep.

Example.

I used to paint a lot of pictures and sell them the following weekend at an art show. Some of the pictures were good. Not all, just some. But of course the best ones sold quickly. And I didn't keep a photographic record of them. I didn't see the point. I just remembered the subject matter and moved on, learning bit by bit what worked and what did not. Some years later along came giclee printing and I was able to make prints of pictures from photographs. But of course I didn't have photographs of all the best stuff.

However, I managed to find a few by going to their owners and borrowing the pictures back for photography. Thank goodness I had kept a record of my sales.

Another artist, who also sold with me at the same venue, did keep good quality slides of all his work. He is now able to call on a vast database of images that will supply him with a supply of prints for years.

Keep good records because you never know when or how they will be used.

There are several photo library computer programmes available, get one. And while you are about it, I recommend that you get a good image-editing programme as well.

Legal issues

You will have to think about your legal status at some stage. Are you going to trade as a sole trader, a partnership, or a limited company?

Your bank manager, solicitor, or financial advisor will help you.

Tax [urgh!]

You will eventually need to engage an accountant who will handle your tax affairs. Ask your local Chamber of Commerce, or business association, or bank manager for advice. Go see the accountant and make sure that he/she understands what sort of business you are going to be, and see if you have a person-to-person rapport. Don't take on an accountant that you don't get on with.

You shouldn't have to pay anything at this stage. But have a meeting and get it arranged at the start, so that you and your accountant, or tax advisor, are singing from the same hymn sheet.

Image

You will need to develop a business image to be reflected in your literature, to be used on business cards and headed notepaper.

You can develop your signature file for email, logo for use on brochures as well.

Chapter Two....Conclusion.

You have been given another two pieces of good news.

- It can be as much fun being an artist in business as just being an artist.
- There is loads of free advice to be had for the asking.

So far you have five golden rules.

GOLDEN RULE No 1:   **INVEST AND BELIEVE IN YOURSELF.**

GOLDEN RULE No 2:   **KEEP RECORDS.**

GOLDEN RULE No 3:   **AIM FOR QUALITY.**

GOLDEN RULE No 4:   **BE BUSINESSLIKE.**

GOLDEN RULE No 5:   **SEEK AND LISTEN TO EXPERT ADVICE.**

GOLDEN RULE No 6:   **?.**

GOLDEN RULE No 7:   **?**

GOLDEN RULE No 8:   **?**

GOLDEN RULE No 9:   **?**

GOLDEN RULE No 10:   **?**

GOLDEN RULE No 11:   **?**

GOLDEN RULE No 12:   **?**

CHAPTER THREE: You choose

In which we discuss choices concerning

your methods,

your subject matter,

your creation style,

and your special market niche.

You probably have had some success and recognition for your art already otherwise you would probably not be thinking about the possibility of being an artist. So your starting point will be from some sort of base. But let us examine other possibilities and not fall into the trap of being blinkered by previous achievements.

Choose your methods.

Methods of painting, printmaking, etc..

There are four main methods of painting, and four more kinds of drawing. They are,

- watercolour
- acrylic
- oils
- pastels
- pen and ink
- pencil
- chalk
- charcoal

There are print making methods including,

- lithography
- silkscreen
- etching
- engraving
- woodcut
- linocut
- giclee

There is sculpture using,
- Clay
- Plaster
- Wood
- Bronze
- Iron
- Stone
- Glass
- Plastic
- Resin

There are wall hangings made from,
- ceramic
- textile
- plaster
- encaustic
- appliqué

There are also,
- photographs
- digital creations
- collage
- montage

There are combinations of any and all these. You have the rest of your lifetime to enjoy exploring as many as you wish.

Choose your subject matter.

Subjects

There are abstracts, landscapes, figures, seascapes, cityscapes, portraits, animals, nudes, dreams, fantasy, still life and many other categories of subject.

Choose your creation style.

Styles

There are dozens of art styles, isms, and schools of art to act as your inspiration. Pre-Raphaelite, impressionism, expressionism, abstract expressionism, dadaism, classicism, surrealism, vorticism, naïve, outsider art, primitive art, futurism, etc. etc etc. The list is a long one, and growing by the minute.

What to choose and where to start.

******* GOOD NEWS .... NUMBER SEVEN ********

There is no need to worry about what you choose from this incredible list, **because they are all good.**

They are all potential routes to your success.

They have all worked for someone or the other in the past.

However, I can point you towards choices that are most likely to fail in today's market place.

Here are a few simple guidelines or 'do not rules' that you may wish to follow or ignore.

- Don't make your art too big. Because you will limit the number of potential users and therefore buyers.
- Don't make your art too scary. Because you will limit the number of potential users and therefore buyers.
- Don't make your art too expensive. Because you will limit the number of potential buyers.

That is too big, too scary, and too expensive. And the thing that they have in common is that they limit the number of potential users and therefore buyers.

What is Big ?

'Big' can mean heavy and demanding as well as large scale. Think about the size of your potential market for something 'big'. It is probably limited to an office reception area, boardroom, airport lounge etc. This is a good lucrative market, but it is well recognised, and lots of people, mostly designers and architects, are after the small number of profitable deals available. However, it is possible to be successful in this area if you get your self noticed by the agencies and specialist dealers who commission and choose this work. The competition is fierce so beware.

What is Scary ?

'Scary' usually means challenging subject matter. The temptation for many new artists to paint surreal dreams and spiky black scenes from the occult dripping in blood should be avoided. I am serious here. I have seen budding artists present portfolios stuffed with this sort of art. It is meant to impress, and it does. But the market is very limited. OK so I actually know an artist who has done very well drawing spiky scary scenes with knights and dramatic visions writhing all over. But I know many many more who have successfully chosen a more popular style and subject matter.

What is expensive?

Too 'expensive' means that your potential customers cannot afford to buy your work. It might mean that you are mistaken about the market rate for your work. Perhaps you suffer from an over-inflated ego and are pricing your work higher than your potential customers think it is worth. Maybe you should ask a few friends whether you are asking too much.

But most probably 'too expensive' results because you have taken too much time doing the work and you are basing your price on the man-hours involved. If it takes a month to paint a picture then you will have only twelve pictures a year to sell. Each one will have to provide one twelfth of your income. If each picture takes three months then you will have to sell each one for a quarter of your projected income. Yikes! But if you can paint one or two or three paintings a week then you can sell them for much less and you will significantly increase your market. It is like pushing string uphill if you try to jump into the art business with very expensive art. That comes later!!

Choose your special market niche.

Market sectors.

The market place for art can be divided up into sectors.

Your family and friends. I strongly advise that you start here, and use the income to support your efforts to expand to other areas after.

Private buyers who buy to hang in their homes. This is the biggest and most likely and potentially profitable sector. So not too big, scary or expensive remember? This sector will buy at exhibitions, in shops, on the doorstep, on holiday, in the shopping mall, on the internet, and wherever they see your stuff.

Private buyers who buy to hang in their workplace. This sector buy extra work that would not fit indoors and use it at their office. Don't ignore this potential market. If you are selling to a customer and spouse you will often hear the comment 'but where will we hang it?'. Don't forget to remind them about the office wall. They don't both have to like it if it is taken to the office.

Corporate buyers who buy for the working environment. This sector is well heeled but the dealers are very aware of the market. Often the buyer will be the interior designer or furnishing specifier. Some big corporations have a dedicated art buyer to find work for their office walls, canteens, corridors etc. Hospitals and hotels use a lot of art. Get in the queue behind the dealers, or get to know the dealers and get them to sell your work. You may get half as much per picture but sell twenty times as many.

As gifts. Gift shops sell low price art objects that people buy as gifts or souvenirs. This market niche is often overlooked even though it has a colossal turnover. Price and 'goods ready to sell' are criteria. In other words it has got to be cheap and the gift shop will not do any framing, packaging or advising. Your work will have to sell itself from the display. Your work might just be the right thing so it would pay to identify this lucrative market.

Dealers who buy to resell to other categories. When you are successful this 'art trade' sector is the most likely market niche for you, because you are a producer, and they are specialist buyers and sellers. But realise and remember that you still have to sell to them of course. They may be art gallery owners, wholesalers or corporate art dealers, or licensing agents. [I assume that this market niche is the one that you will target sooner or later as your art career develops. If you choose not to sell to the art trade, then you are either mad or very fortunate. Please let me know. It might be the subject of another book.]

Investors who buy to make a profit later. I suggest that you do not target this market niche because realistically it applies in only a very few instances. However, you would be very shrewd to remember that the 'invest to make profit' mind-set is a major secondary reason to buy. Buyers in other categories might well make buying decisions because the extra element of long-term profit seems a real possibility.

Licensors. These are those who buy to use the art in other formats, e.g. greetings cards, calendars, tee-shirts, etc. This sector is growing rapidly. There are specialist agents who can hunt out deals for your art in far-flung corners of the world, and for the most unlikely purposes. I reckon that you should get established in other areas first but keep in touch with this market especially if you make art that is popular in other areas.

Publishers who buy to reproduce and sell as posters or limited edition prints. Publishers have had a massive influence on the available choice of pictures and prints hanging on people's walls for the last hundred years. They still represent the most likely source for most artwork in people's homes. The growth of print technology has lead to artists self-publishing. This has been the astonishing phenomenon of the last five or six years. It has had a profound impact on this sector. See more later.

Patrons, well-wishers, art lovers, fairy godmothers, and lunatics. Best of luck with this sector. Do not rely on it. Don't even think it might happen. You have got to make it without patronage, or the generosity and altruism of people who think you are a good artist. The exception being those in category one, family and friends. These are in limited supply.

Chapter Three.....Conclusion

You will have seen that the title of this book is 'How to Make a Living as an Artist' and NOT 'How to paint pictures'. Maybe that book will come later! Our focus in this volume is on the practical techniques [competence], and mental mindset [confidence] required to be an artist. You can paint or sculpt what and how you want. Do it as well as you can of course. Remember the third golden rule 'Aim for Quality'.

This chapter has looked at the variety of choices available, and emphasised that there is no one right choice.

So now you can focus on a method for your art, a style for your art, and a target market for your art. Keep your choice, and focus, down to one of each to start. Although you will probably have a second choice style, method and market target for your further attention, should your first choice prove to be the wrong one, or you are successful and wish to expand.

So far you have five golden rules. There are no new golden rules in the choice of art method, subject or style because it is possible that you can succeed with any combination. There are no golden rules about which niche to aim at. There are guidelines to help you choose.

However it is very important that you do choose a style, method, subject area, and a market niche to target first. So here is another golden rule,

---

GOLDEN RULE No 6: FOCUS YOUR EFFORT

Focusing on your target or task is crucial. Try brainstorming with a trusted friend or partner. Try using mind-maps to help you look all round the problem and free yourself from assumption traps.

That makes six golden rules to carry forward,

GOLDEN RULE No 1:   **INVEST AND BELIEVE IN YOURSELF.**

GOLDEN RULE No 2:   **KEEP RECORDS.**

GOLDEN RULE No 3:   **AIM FOR QUALITY.**

GOLDEN RULE No 4:   **BE BUSINESSLIKE.**

GOLDEN RULE No 5:   **SEEK AND LISTEN TO EXPERT ADVICE.**

GOLDEN RULE No 6:   **FOCUS YOUR EFFORT.**

GOLDEN RULE No 7:   **?**

GOLDEN RULE No 8:   **?**

GOLDEN RULE No 9:   **?**

GOLDEN RULE No 10:   **?**

GOLDEN RULE No 11:   **?**

GOLDEN RULE No 12:   **?**

CHAPTER FOUR: Who wants to buy my work?

Finding your customers and collectors.

In this chapter we outline 8 strategies for approaching the targets for your sales effort.

There are two ways of finding your end user customers.

- Those that you find directly yourself (this chapter)
- Those that you find indirectly through the fine art trade (next chapter)

The first way, that is doing it yourself, **DIY**, must be your primary choice.

Remember that your first priority is, SURVIVAL.

The benefits of finding your own customers are many-fold.

- You get to keep all the money
- You meet the buyers and find out who they are
- You get feed back and other comments from the buyers
- The buyers get to meet you and that builds loyalty

So let us concentrate on the direct method first. Remember that reason number one is that it is going to earn you a bigger percentage, [that is unless you spend a fortune finding the customers, so be careful].

DIY Target 1: Family, friends and neighbours.

This is where the low hanging fruit is ripe for plucking.

Just ask your family, friends, neighbours, and acquaintances to buy your pictures please. Let them know that you are now a professional artist and that you really want them to get in on the ground floor while prices are low and that you will always appreciate their help in getting you started. Engage them if possible to help sell to other members of the family and their friends and their friend's families and their friends families friends etc.. This word of mouth, family loyalty, friends and neighbours solidarity is a gold mine that you should not ignore.

Take on board all the comments and suggestions that will come your way. In fact ask for comments and suggestions, but don't act on all of them. This pool of goodwill and advice could point you in the right direction.

The longest journey starts with the first step. Don't be too proud to get all the help you can get at this stage. Be blatant, beg, plead, and be eternally grateful for every little word of interest and encouragement. Don't be disheartened by the doubters, or people that tell you to go away and learn to be a doctor or a lawyer. They are thinking short term.

Point out to them that Picasso died and left his family £650 million [that is over $1,000,000.000]. The wealthiest artist alive today, said to be Thomas Kinkade, has an annual turnover in millions of dollars.

DIY Targets 2 and 3. Finding and Selling to Private buyers who buy to hang in their homes and workplace.

Strategy No 1. Door to door.

Do you know how I paid my way through art school? I was a poor student living in a rundown rented apartment in the poor side of town. I was married with two babies. I needed more money than my student grant provided. So I got a dozen old picture frames from a junk shop, took out the faded prints inside, painted new pictures the right size to fit the frames, put the whole thing back together, and put them into the babies pram one evening and set off walking to a new housing development a few blocks away.

I knocked on the first door and said, " Hello, I am an artist and I am trying to sell my paintings. Would you like to have a look?" It took another couple of doors before I found an interested looker. But it worked. I went home two hours later with a week's wages in cash in my pocket.

I later built up a business employing eight people based on the same principle. We had four light vans that went out every weekend, each with a two-man crew and a stock of ready to hang original paintings. We chose areas of new development, new housing estates and owner occupied housing.

The method was simple. I would carry two pictures, knock on the first door in a row of houses and step back one pace when the door was opened. I would smile, make honest eye contact, and say, 'Hallo. I am an artist and I am trying to sell my paintings;'then pause, smile again, let it sink in. Then ask 'Would you like to have a look?'. Believe me it worked.

About one in ten said yes and either took me in there and then, or made a date for a subsequent visit. When I was invited into a potential buyer's home this is what I did

I took in about fifteen pictures and displayed them on the floor leaning up against the furniture or walls.

I asked a few simple questions like 'where do you want to hang something new?'

I remembered that 'silence is pressure' and waited with my mouth shut during the long pauses when the potential customer was thinking about my pictures or wishing that I would go away.

I let the pictures speak for them selves and I didn't make the classic mistake of talking the customer away from the sale.

I learnt to look and wait for the moment in time when I could make an assumption that the viewer was willing to become a buyer.

I learnt to listen to the customers and make notes about their reactions.

I valued their input into my art.

I saw what was working, and what was not, in terms of communication of my artistic idea.

It is a bit daunting for a single female to present herself to complete strangers and accept invitations to go into their homes. But Ihave worked with some brave and confident women who have used this approach very well without any harm.

Strategy No 2. Open air exhibition

OK so you don't want to do all that knocking on doors.

So how about an open-air exhibit along a fence somewhere?

Many tourist places have such a show. If not why not start your own. Find a suitable backdrop, with plenty of walking traffic, get permission from the owners where possible, and just put up your stuff. Eventually the authorities and other businesses in the area will come to realise that you are an attraction, and will be positive in their dealings with a well run open-air art show.

I sold my very first painting while still a student at the annual Embankment show in London which was held for a couple of weeks in Temple Gardens behind the Strand Hotel. Sadly that show has long since ceased to be.

Later in my career I exhibited for many years every Sunday in London where a couple of such street markets still thrive. They are at Bayswater

Road along the north of Hyde Park, and Piccadilly along the north side of Green Park.

At shows like this, artists come from many miles away and hang art on allotted pitches and sell to passers by. The competition is hot, the prices are low, and it gets cold in the winter.

However I can tell you that a lot of artists have made small fortunes doing this.

Big houses, yachts, nice cars, holidays and luxurious weekday lifestyle, are not the only benefits. You will learn to paint what people want, at a price that people want to pay, and you will be building up a mailing list of collectors that could stand you in good stead for many years after you cease to exhibit on the fence. [Golden Rule No 2: Keep Records]

Strategy No 3. Indoor exhibitions

Or how about developing the previous ideas and doing the same indoors at your local shopping mall or community hall. You want somewhere cheap that does not expect to take a percentage of your sales. The attraction is that the passers by will be meeting the artist and able to buy directly from them.

A variation on this theme happened in my hometown in recent years. A group of artists found empty shops that were waiting to be re-let. They approached the owners and managed to get temporary lets at peppercorn rents in exchange for clearing out the old fixtures, and repainting the interior in white. The group advertised themselves as ConTEMPORARY Art Exhibitions.

A similar group found derelict factory and office buildings and converted them into studios and galleries. Eventually, after developing the expertise and getting a track record, the group obtained huge funds and bought a complete office building, which now houses 30 to 40 studios and a superb gallery space.

Strategy No 4. Art parties

Canadian artist Michael Tickner tells the story of his road to success and recognition using a series of home exhibitions hosted in collectors homes.

" I chose host houses where the host already had an example of my artwork. Together with the host we would invite as many people as possible. We made a map showing how to get to the house. The host addressed the envelopes and sent out the invites two weeks before the *exhibition day. We had the 'private view' on a Thursday between 7pm and 10 pm.*

On the day I would show up at 10 am, and spend time moving furniture around so that we exhibited in two or three rooms. I supplied all the lights and easels for the display. We printed a catalogue with titles, details and prices of the art. The paintings were numbered to match the catalogue. We gave this printed sheet of paper to all visitors to take away. It included my address and contact number and a message from me.

I provided wine, music, and cheesy nibbles.

The host provided space and customers.

Our split was 75% to me and 25% to the host payable in paintings. The host was thus able to get another picture from me by selling three to her friends.

We had a special treat for our potential buyers who showed an interest in a particular picture. We had an unoccupied easel in the hall or somewhere in a prominent position. We had arranged a spotlight that was on a dimmer switch. We moved the painting onto the empty easel and turned up the dimmer switch. Wow! Everybody waited for the buyer to decide, which they usually did there and then."

Strategy No 5. Juried Artshows.

In the USA there are many established art shows where painters and photographers can exhibit and sell directly to the public. Greg Lawler's Art Fair Source Book is a superb guide to more than 600 art shows, art fairs, and festivals. It includes listings, guides, rules, costs, reviews and ratings. See www.artfairsourcebook.com

Reading the reviews is well worthwhile. You can find out about the kind of thing that interests the erstwhile exhibitor, such as parking, set up and break down problems, weather, sales price guide, and costs.

A very good article on exhibiting and selling photography at art shows in USA can be found in the May 2003 Shutterbug Magazine. The author Larry Berman is a photographer who has sold at art shows for over 25 years. The article can be found on his website: www.artshowphoto.com

Larry has given permission for his experience to be included here. In the following article you will see that many of his tips are applicable to artists in other sectors of the art world. The site is well worth a visit! Here is a flavour of his interesting information.

Applying to an Art Show

How to find an art show to apply to

Most exhibitors hear about shows from other exhibitors. It's like a closed community. I've seen a lot of the same people exhibiting for over 25 years. On the other hand, it's really interesting to see new and different work being exhibited so I feel that there is always room for newcomers.

*Aside from the individual state art listings, there are two important resources that give you the information needed to obtain an application for specific shows and how those shows rank on a national level. The first and most important is the **Art Fair Sourcebook**, put together by the veteran art show photographer Greg Lawler. The book is published annually and is an expensive but necessary resource if you're considering art shows as a profession. It lists the top 300 art shows in the country with an in-depth look at their requirements and feedback comments that have been accumulated by the author. The other is **Sunshine Artist Magazine**, which is the closest thing there is to a trade magazine in the art show business. There are show reports listed by state, and the rear contains a listing of art show contact information that is listed by location and date. There are also advertisements throughout the magazine for companies that sell products that are used by art show exhibitors. If you're just beginning, a subscription to this magazine is a must read.*

The first thing to consider is the application. Most art shows mail out their applications six to eight months in advance. It lists their requirements for admission and for display. It also lists the quantity of slides required, how to prepare the slides, the fees to enclose (both booth and application fee), the date it has to be postmarked by and the SASE (self-addressed stamped envelope). Some applications have room for a description of your work, either generally or by slide. You can't just call up a show at the last minute and ask for a space. The show has invited a group of "experts" to jury the submitted slides on a preset date. But don't expect feedback on your work. Currently the art shows just put your slides in your SASE with a form letter telling you that you haven't been accepted but to feel free to apply again next year.

Not to disillusion you, but there are shows that I've been accepted to after applying to for over ten years. But those top shows maintain their reputation and the sales have made it worthwhile for the ten years of jury fees. If you're serious about selling your photography at art shows as a source of income, I recommend maintaining a list of the top shows and applying to them every year. Even though it's almost like playing the lottery, if you can produce a high quality of imagery, you have a *chance of being accepted at some point. That's how I approach the business. [**Larry Berman**]*

Strategy No 6. Online galleries

Here is another idea. It is new with a short track record.

Sell on line through your website, or through any one of the proliferation of on line galleries. As a start you should avoid spending any real money by doing as much as possible yourself. Get a cheap website host and design a simple website yourself showing your work. Inform your viewers how to contact you by phone or email.

No need to spend a lot of money developing a shopping cart in the early stages. Invite your viewers to get in touch by phone or email to begin with.

Tell everybody about it and submit to search engines using all the key words that describe your art.

 Submit to free galleries and a selection of reasonable pay for exposure galleries if you want to.

You will need to take credit cards so get your self a merchant account with Visa, MasterCard and American Express.

My own website sells my pictures steadily. Maybe one or two paintings or prints a week. With a bit more time and effort spent on promotion it could do much more.

Strategy No 7. Online auction houses like e-bay.

Brett Raven has written a very successful e-book that tells how he has sold his art on eBay. I include it here because he has so much experience in this area. Here is what he says about his book.

'This powerful little ebook will pay for itself with the sale of your first work of art! Secure your position as a successful Ebay artist and start earning money! This ebook isn't boring as some information books may be; feeding you a bunch of rambling junk. I get straight to the point, giving you the most important facts; that is why it may seem like a small book with only 16 pages, but it delivers a punch! That I promise. There is no other place on the entire internet with the information found in this ebook. You can scour the internet for weeks and you still won't come close finding all of the valuable tips and strategies contained within this ebook. Take my 4 years of experience and compress it into one day of reading! Don't make the mistakes that so many unsuccessful artists make. Earn money from home. List your art using my strategies and you

could possibly see results that very day. Won't you join me on Ebay?"
[**Brett Raven**]

Click here to get Brett's book:

http://hop.clickbank.net/?crabfish/ebayartist

Open house or studio.

Oh yes, and then there are open studios and open houses.

This method of finding customer/collectors is a very old method indeed. An artist operating from a studio in Italy or Holland, hundreds of years ago, would invite patrons into his workplace to see work in progress. Often the artist would have a separate raised area looking down onto the dirty studio floor, where apprentices would be grinding pigment and mixing paint, so that the clients could see and not get dirty themselves. The artist would show his work in this clean area and get commissions or sales from the visitor. This area was the 'gallery', a term since borrowed by art shops and dealers.

Showing your clients your working and living secrets has been effective ever since. So make an occasion out of it. Set aside a special day and invite them in. Give them a nibble or a drink if possible. Have the prices written down in advance, preferably at a good rate that takes into account the lack of commission to pay to dealers. This will give the visitors a good reason to buy from you there and then. Put labels on, or next to, the pictures with details like title, medium, size and price. Or number the pictures and print a hand-held list with the details against each number. This list should include your contact details in case the visitors take it away with them.

It is worthwhile considering joining forces with other artists to make a bigger occasion out of it. Here in my hometown, Brighton UK, there is an annual Festival during which about 250 artists open their doors and exhibit work by about 1000 artists and craftsmen. This draws a crowd of some 100,000 visitors. No I have not made this up! The turnover in direct business must be colossal. You can see more about this here:

www.fivewaysartists.com

And don't forget to get a visitors book and ask for names and addresses for your mailing list.

GOLDEN RULE No 7: JOIN UP, MEET PEOPLE, NETWORK.

The life of an artist can be rather lonely and insular because you are usually in your studio alone. This golden rule suggests that you join up with other artists to share ideas and selling opportunities, meet people on as many occasions as possible to spread the word about yourself and your work, and network with your trade organisations, art groups, neighbourhood groups, and anywhere where you can make contacts. It is often about whom you know not what you know!

Chapter Four .... Conclusion

You should start the business of selling your art by selecting target markets that you can sell to on your own.

We have shown you 8 possible strategies.

You will get a much bigger percentage of the retail sales income, and you will get direct feedback from the customers who you will meet face to face.

GOLDEN RULE No 1:   **INVEST AND BELIEVE IN YOURSELF.**

GOLDEN RULE No 2:   **KEEP RECORDS.**

GOLDEN RULE No 3:   **AIM FOR QUALITY.**

GOLDEN RULE No 4:   **BE BUSINESSLIKE.**

GOLDEN RULE No 5:   **SEEK AND LISTEN TO EXPERT ADVICE.**

GOLDEN RULE No 6:   **FOCUS YOUR EFFORT.**

GOLDEN RULE No 7:   **JOIN UP, MEET PEOPLE, NETWORK.**

GOLDEN RULE No 8:   **?**

GOLDEN RULE No 9:   **?**

GOLDEN RULE No 10:   **?**

GOLDEN RULE No 11:   **?**

GOLDEN RULE No 12:   **?**

CHAPTER FIVE: From survival to success

In which we look at selling to the fine art trade

And give you four nasty shocks

Target 4. Corporate buyers who buy for the working environment.

You will find this market niche difficult to control yourself. There are specialist dealers and agencies set up to satisfy buyers and specifiers who choose pictures for corporate use. Many corporate customers will demand a framed, delivered, and hung service, with art for rent or purchase contract.

They might expect the art in their office/restaurant/hospital/etc. to be changed every now and then. It has to be safely hung and framed to a very high standard to avoid costly litigation should a cord break or glass smash.

Make yourself known to agents in this business. However it is still possible to find some business in this sector yourself, especially locally.

Your website should offer this sector the possibility of using your pictures.

Target 5. As items for the gift trade.

The gift market can be very seasonal with a huge surge in the weeks running up to Christmas. If you make an art product that is the right price and suitable for gifts, then examine this sector very carefully.

Impulse buying is going to be the key process. You will have to provide a ready to go and hang item. Bagged with cord and wall hangings perhaps. Smaller items that can be gift wrapped and carried away will do much better than bigger items.

However there are some interesting exceptions to this rule. I had a commission recently for a portrait of a young couple just about to be married. They liked my work but could not afford an original. So they wrote to all their wedding guests and invited them to send a donation directly to me for the proposed portrait. The total came to more than the cost of the picture and they were able to commission a series of greetings cards based on the picture as well.

Another variation in this sector involves the many tourists and holidaymakers who buy art when on vacation. They might be buying for them selves or as gifts for family and friends when they get home.

The advice about making ready to hang packages applies here, although sometimes buyers can be worried about long homeward return journeys with glass. If you are in a tourist area why not find where they congregate and set up a sales outlet with yourself in attendance, They will love meeting the artist, and you will benefit by the interaction and feedback that they give you. Remember to take records of their names addresses and email contacts. This pool of customers can be re-fished at a later date.

You will probably have to think about exhibiting at a specialist trade fair to meet the buyers in this sector. See more later.

Target 6. Dealers who buy to resell.

When you are a little more successful you will be in demand so much that you will need to share your selling with dealers. They will probably have gallery premises to sell to the end user. Or they may be wholesale dealers who will sell to galleries. Other categories are the dealers who sell to the corporate market, or licensing and publishing market.

A nasty shock, number one.

Your biggest shock will be the same shock that all artists get when they delve into this market for the first time.

You will only get a small percentage of the gallery selling price for yourself.

A picture, painting or print will sell at four or five times the amount that you will get if you expect other parties to do all the selling.

Here is an example of the way it works,

An artist paints a picture on canvas and asks for £50 from a friendly local gallery that he or she knows already. The gallery will usually want to sell at 100% mark-up, which would mean a selling price of £100 plus tax. Galleries have high overheads and staff costs so don't expect them to take less. The gallery will probably want to reframe the picture to reflect the taste of the established gallery clientele. So they might charge the customer another £50 for the frame. You the artist will see the painting nicely framed in the gallery window for £175 and could be dismayed that you only get £50.

Now see what happens if you use a middleman dealer to sell to all the other non-local galleries that you do not know. Once again you must expect the dealer to want a 100% mark-up. So your picture will go from you at £50, and then from the middleman at £100 and from the gallery at £200, plus new frame and tax, making it have a £275 price tag for the end-user. That is over five-times mark-up from your price. Or, another way to see it, you will get under 20% of the eventual selling price.

To make it worse you will have a lot of pressure from the other parties in this chain to drop your price because £275 is too high for something that you originally valued at £50. Halve your asking price to £25 and the eventual selling price is still something like £175 because the framing costs the same.

So you will have to paint a picture worth £275 and get just £50!

Trade Fairs.

Let me make it even worse for a moment before I make it better.

A nasty shock, number two.

If you wish to find the dealers who will market your work, you might have to spend a lot of effort and money showing at a trade fair.

This is going to cost you a small fortune.

In the UK a very small stand at the Spring Fair or the Autumn Fair in Birmingham will probably cost over £2000, if you can get in. There is a waiting list for the Spring Fair.

Plus your lighting costs, which you will think are extortionate. [To rent a single spotlight for the five day Fair is about the same cost as buying one, but you don't keep the light.] You will be asked to pay for all these well in advance.

On top of this is your hotel cost, maybe plus your van hire, plus your brochure etc..

But you will probably have to take a stand at a Fair like this if you want to make sure that you are noticed and taken seriously by the dealers, middlemen and retailers who attend.

A similar Fair in the USA is ArtExpo at the Jacob Javitts Centre in New York every March, and another in Atlanta in September. The cost is similar, but at least in New York you have an opportunity to recoup some of your expenditure, because the Fair is open to the general public for some of the time. This is when you have a chance to sell direct at something approaching full retail price.

A nasty shock, number three.

Trade fair exposure can take several years to take effect and pay off.

The Fine Art Trade Guild in London hold a briefing seminar for UK exhibitors who are going to the New York ArtExpo show. In this seminar the Guild give new exhibitors the well-researched advice that they should budget for a three-year exhibiting plan before the likelihood of making a profit.

The UK government support new exporters at some trade fairs including the ArtExpo in New York and another in Atlanta later in the year. The UK government and the Guild also support/sponsor the SACA show in Italy, where you might get noticed by the European market. This support consists mainly of a grant for half the stand cost less a management fee. This could save you a couple of thousand pounds if you are eligible. Never-the-less, the cost of doing a trade fair at home or abroad is still high.

The upside to this big risky expenditure is that, if it works, several retail galleries will notice you, any of which could be your chief customers for many years ahead. Plus you might make contact with a middleman agency who could handle all your selling from then on. Plus the major publishers will see you, and you will be in all the show catalogues, which will be in use for the next year at least.

An alternative to trade fairs that can be done on a shoestring.

The alternative to a huge and risky capital outlay is, once again simply put, **'do it yourself'**. You do this by visiting the gallery or dealer personally.

That means a lot of research, preparation, legwork, and sales technique. You will need to find out,

- Where target galleries or dealers are based.
- Who is the decision maker?
- When he/she is willing to look at your portfolio.
- What he/she is looking for.
- How he/she wishes to be dealt with.
- Why they should be interested in your work instead of the hundreds of other hopefuls who knock on the door every week.

GOLDEN RULE No 8: BE PREPARED, TURN UP.

This is a very important golden rule. Get yourself ready by thinking ahead and rehearsing what you are going to do.

Think and rehearse success.
And then make sure that you turn up.

[There is more about turning up in Chapter Seven.]

You will also have to prepare your sales pitch. You will have to have a realistic price list. You will need a biography and other selling information for the end-user customer to mull over. This might include a statement about your art and a photograph or two showing you working in your studio.

- You should make an appointment to meet the gallery decision maker who might not be the owner.

- You should be pleasant and businesslike in your approach.

- Always make absolutely sure that you are on time.

- Have your work very well prepared for the showing.

- Do not try to show too much on your first meeting.

- Be prepared to make more than one visit before the gallery offers you any kind of deal.

- Listen to what the gallery contact says about your work.

- Ask advice from the gallery contact.

- Ask for leads to other galleries who might be interested in your type of work. This will be a very good introduction if you can get it. You will have much more likelihood of reaching the right person, who could be in the right frame of mind, if you come by recommendation.

- Be prepared to try several galleries before you get a positive response.

Many galleries will have a client base built up over the years largely interested in a particular type of work, usually influenced by the taste of the proprietor. The chances are that your work will not to fit. You could have found out this before you go to the gallery and not made the effort of course. But, hey, you are there, maybe the gallery contact doesn't like your work, and it could all have been a huge waste of time and effort. But, if you ask the gallery contact for a lead, or even a word of mouth introduction, you might find a way to another more suitable contact after all.

When you find a gallery that does like your work, then this is your big opportunity to get leads to other galleries. If the gallery contact wishes to stock your work then his/her taste will have also selected the other artists on show. Find out about other galleries that stock those artists and approach them. You could ask the artists, you could ask the gallery, you could search the internet, you could ask your trade association, or you could scour old copies of gallery listing magazines and look for artists that do the same genre of work as yourself.

A nasty shock, number four.

Ah, but then you have another rude awakening!

The gallery will not buy your work outright

That is unless they know you, and to be brutally frank, they have no other choice. They will want it on consignment, or on a sale-or-return basis, or for an exhibition only.

So be prepared to be asked to produce a body of work, that you will have to frame to very high standards, and then provide this to the gallery at some future date, and then wait for a long time before the gallery eventually tells you that they have sold something. Then, and not until then, can you send the gallery an invoice for the goods sold. Then wait another thirty days to get paid.

A way to attract dealers to you is to provide prints or greetings cards as well as originals. Prints or cards are possibly going to be your main earner in many venues. Galleries are much more likely to buy prints or cards because the risk per unit is a lot less. You might have to guarantee that you will exchange anything that does not attract sufficient custom or remains unsold.

Advertising.

You could try to put advertisements in the trade press.

In the UK there are two art and picture business trade magazines.

They are called; wait for it....

The Picture Business [TPB], and **Art Business Today** [ABT].

www.picturebusiness.uk.com

The ABT is published by The Fine Art Trade Guild, which is your friendly worldwide trade organization based in the UK.

www.fineart.co.uk

TBP is published by emap, who are a multi interest concern, and who amongst many other things, own the aforementioned Spring and Autumn Fairs in Birmingham.

In the USA a similar publication is **Art Business News** and is published by Advanstar Communications Inc.

www.artbusinessnews.com

An advert with something like 'starving artist of international reputation seeks agents and galleries to share the profits' might just work. I haven't tried it myself, neither will I, unless you do and it makes you famous. Remember it was my idea.

Editorial

Far more effective is to get free editorial coverage in these same trade magazines. You will need to have a good interesting and pertinent story to tell. The story must be of use to the readership. And the editor will not add your sales pitch clincher in the story. The sales pitch clincher is the part of the message that informs the reader what to do next, which in your case might be 'phone and put in your order'. So always ask the editor to add an email address or phone number so that you can be contacted.

Mail-shot.

You could always try a mail-shot. You will need to get hold of a good list. Businesses using 'mail-shot-selling' buy lists from list sellers. But it is possible to compile a list yourself by combing through the yellow pages or trade directories. The Fine Art Trade Guild directory has names and addresses for hundreds of galleries and middlemen agents in the UK. Similar directories will be available in other countries from trade organizations and chambers of commerce.

Your mail-shot should include good quality images and price lists, and of course your 'unique selling point' as mentioned elsewhere in this book.

Target 7. Investors who buy to make a profit later.

There are a number of buyers throughout the world who have made a significant profit by buying and selling art as an investment. The art market in secondary art, that is second hand art in lay-mans terms, is well established for old masters, contemporary art, and original prints. One of the centres for this is London and another NewYork.

There are a number of top galleries who buy work with the idea that they will sell to national collections for the national art bank.

There are a number of lesser galleries who buy work to sell to the top galleries.

There are even lesser dealers who sell to those galleries, and individuals who try to play the market.

How does this affect you as a possible professional artist? If you are reading this book, then probably not at all. If you have not been snapped up while still young and at a major prestigious art college, then it is probably too late to hope to be in this market. The dealers favour a few students each year. Put them under contract and then spit out the ones who do not conform. The spat out ones will end up teaching back in those same prestigious art colleges. Ye Gods, I am cynical about this aren't I?

The exception might be someone like Grandma Moses or another such late developing naïf such as Alfred Wallace, or even Lowry. Most of the non-trained artists who hit the big league do so after they die. Thus the market is making absolutely sure that there is a controllable supply and demand, which will ensure high prices.

This is very unsavoury territory.

Target 8. Licensors.

The licensing sector is growing fast. The use of art in other near and not so near industries is often supplied by licensing agreements. The artist allows an image to be used for say greetings cards or calendars and gets a royalty or down payment from the manufacturer in return. Art has been used for many years in the ceramics industry, and the book and magazine publishing industries. But now art can be seen on coasters, tee shirts, luggage, jigsaw puzzles, furnishings, in advertising, record covers, and many more uses.

We have devoted a whole chapter to this sector, see chapter ten.

Target 9. Publishers

Art publishers also deserve a whole chapter to them selves, see chapter nine.

Target 10. Patrons, well-wishers, art lovers, fairy godmothers, and lunatics.

Oh dear! This sector of the art market is where you can find all those who don't really fit into any of the previous target areas. This list, patrons, well-wishers, art lovers, fairy godmothers, and lunatics, are legitimate customers who merit attention. They nearly all buy art.

Let us look at them one by one.

Patrons.

There is something in some successful businessmen and women that seems to push them towards patronage of the arts. They like art, they have done well in life themselves, or they inherited wealth, and they want to be patrons. They want to be patrons, they want to be patrons, they want to be patrons. Get it? They like the idea of patronage because it makes them feel good, about themselves. There is prestige in being a patron.

You as an artist can benefit from this. But you are being patronised.

It is possible to seek out patronage and exploit it. Many art institutions rely on patronage for their incomes and provide status grooming in return. Maybe you will be able to recognise a potential patron when you bump into one, and maybe you should nurture the budding patron wherever possible. It is up to you.

Patronage in some states of the USA is encouraged by tax breaks for the patron. What a good idea!

Well wishers.

These guys are nicer to deal with than patrons. But hey, maybe they are the same thing as each other. Maybe patrons are well wishers gone bad or something. Anyway I reckon that you can deal with well wishers because you can look 'em in the eye and give something in return, such as a good deal on a painting or something. You can find them if you ask around easily enough. You will find that non-artist folk are very respectful of the humble artist trying his/her best. Especially if you are not doing very well at the start of your dedicated career. Well wishers can be asked for simple help in such things as exhibition space, printing brochures, cheap premises, even housing. They will enjoy helping you out and you can make their lives more exciting by sharing some artistic ambition or insight. They can be good customers too. Treat each one with the same care and tenderness that you would a young tender plant or a newborn chick that could turn out to be a golden goose.

Art lovers.

These can be a bit of a handful because they will often know more about art history than you. You might feel a bit of a fraud when someone else who isn't an actual artist tells you that Rembrandt used such and such type of varnish and hand ground pigments, and what do you use? They can be another source of private collector if you hit it off with them. If you have an open studio then you will get them coming to see you. Unfortunately they often seem to have a very full house themselves and cannot find any more room for your art. Hey ho. Why not look for the younger ones and nurture them into becoming one of your well wishing collectors.

Fairy Godmothers.

You might just come across one of these if you get up very early before anyone else and very carefully watch the saucer of milk that you left out in your studio the night before. Oh yes, and pigs might fly.

Lets admit it, there are not any fairy godmothers. You are going to have to work out your own way to get to the ball.

> ### GOLDEN RULE NUMBER 9: DON'T EXPECT FAIRY GODMOTHERS.
>
> You probably know by now that the tooth fairy and Father Christmas were invented by grown ups. Now you are grown up as well. So be realistic and make it work without the aid of any fairy godmother. Give up hoping that others will do your work for you. Only you can make it, or fail it.

Lunatics.

On the other hand there are a few lunatics around who seem to be art buyers for none of the other aforementioned reasons. Unfortunately I cannot tell you how to find or avoid them. Be very prepared to pounce, or run, whenever the species turns up. But also beware they might just be artists pretending to be customers. The difference between artists and lunatics is very difficult to tell in bad light.

Chapter Five......Conclusion

This chapter was the big one. When you move from survival to success you will be selling to the art business. But there are some nasty shocks for the new comer.

These are the golden rules that you should know by now.

GOLDEN RULE No 1:　　　**INVEST AND BELIEVE IN YOURSELF.**

GOLDEN RULE No 2:　　　**KEEP RECORDS.**

GOLDEN RULE No 3:　　　**AIM FOR QUALITY.**

GOLDEN RULE No 4:　　　**BE BUSINESSLIKE.**

GOLDEN RULE No 5:　　　**SEEK AND LISTEN TO EXPERT ADVICE.**

GOLDEN RULE No 6:　　　**FOCUS YOUR EFFORT.**

GOLDEN RULE No 7:　　　**JOIN UP, MEET PEOPLE, NETWORK.**

GOLDEN RULE No 8:　　　**BE PREPARED, TURN UP.**

GOLDEN RULE No 9:　　　**DON'T EXPECT FAIRY GODMOTHERS.**

GOLDEN RULE No 10　　　**;?**

GOLDEN RULE No 11:　　　**?**

GOLDEN RULE No 12:　　　**?**

CHAPTER SIX: Showing off

Exhibiting your work.

OK, so you are focused and prepared and you have a plan, and you have some art. You have shown your work in your home or studio to all the people on your mailing list. You have trawled around the local galleries, and talked to all the dealers and gallery personnel that you can find. You have opened an internet account and designed your own website where your work is shown to the world.

Q. What's next?

A. How about exhibiting your work.

Of course you will have noticed that many artists have curriculum vitae with a long list of exhibitions. This is impressive and gives potential buyers a lot of confidence in your work.

There are several kinds of exhibition, and they differ quite a lot in value to your CV. And they differ a lot more in real value to you.

>A one-man show in a hired gallery.

>An art group show.

>An open mixed show in a non-profit venue.

>A juried mixed show in a public gallery.

>A mixed show in a commercial gallery

>A two or three man show in a commercial gallery.

>A one-man show in a commercial gallery.

>A one-man show in a prestigious public institution or museum.

A one man show in a hired gallery.

One option is for you to buy your way in. You might be tempted to invest some hard earned profit or savings on gallery space for hire. Galleries that rent out their premises and allow you to put up your own exhibition in dedicated arty surroundings are available all over. My usual advice is ....do not do this!

Any gallery that rents out space will have a changing exhibition about once a fortnight. So twice a month, every month, a new unknown artist is available to the public. This sounds as though it should be a good thing. After all the gallery have told you that they will charge you rent and a low commission, or even no commission, instead of the normal gallery commission haven't they. They even offer to let you use their mailing list to send your invitations as well. Ah-ha! Here is the clue. This is why I don't reckon that this is a good idea. The really good thing about exhibiting in a **good** gallery is that the gallery will have a mailing list of educated and dedicated collectors.

Here is that 80/20 rule again, for galleries. It is probably something like this...**80% of sales in the gallery will be to the 20% of people who have visited and spoken to the sales staff previously, and have been invited to private views of new exhibitions. That means that the other 80% of visitors buy only 20% of the art.**

The gallery will have built up a relationship between gallery staff and customers over a period of time. The list will be nurtured, and lovingly tended, and lots of time and effort will have been lavished on maintaining it. It is guarded jealously and very precious, because the list is the lifeblood of a good gallery.

So anybody who offers to lend you a mailing list is just lending you an inferior list gleaned from the telephone directory. Any gallery that foregoes their 50% commission when they sell one of your pieces must be suspect. They are not going to try very hard!

Here is the truth about gallery space for hire. The gallery owner is making his/her profit by charging you rent. They will not have spent time and money building up a list of good customers. Renting gallery space is only worthwhile if you already have a good list of keen buyers that you have built up yourself, and you are going to man the show all the time it is open, and do all the selling.

An art group exhibition.

An art group show can be your first public experience. You should explore the local art group scene and certainly apply to join a group who have a regular and well run show. The show will probably be once a year. You will not get a lot of space because all group members will be after the same thing.

Prices at an art group show will be lower than the commercial marketplace and you are likely to be next to an enthusiastic amateur with no commercial acumen. The price competition will be fierce, the standard of painting and presentation might be poor, and the visitors will be friends and relatives of the artists. But if the show is held in a good area, and has been well run for some years previously, and will be manned by keen sales-people, and the publicity machinery and private viewing etc. are well done.... then you could just sell a few pieces.

You will learn a great deal in your first show because you can ask your art group elders to help and guide you through. You will be able to interest your family and friends who will certainly come to the free wine and cheese private view. This is your chance to sell to your target sector number one isn't it?

An open mixed show in a non-profit venue.

Your local library, or town hall, or similar institution, might arrange mixed shows that look like the group shows discussed already. The difference being that the show is open to all comers, not just a particular group. Keep your eyes and ears open for these chances. The entry costs shouldn't be high, the commission taken will be bearable, and the selling expertise will be pretty dire. But it can be an opportunity to network with others and get some exposure, and learn a bit more about the business that you are in.

A juried mixed show in a public gallery.

A juried show is a bit more prestigious and a bit more difficult to get in. You will probably have to submit slides or photographs of your work and provide a resume. Your initial effort here is to avoid being seen as an amateur who will let the side down. [See Larry Berman in Chapter 4].

A mixed show in a commercial gallery.

So how do you get into a commercial gallery? These galleries are trying to make a profit from sales of artists work. But they will not be sure about your work until they have built up a following for you, It might take a couple of mixed exhibitions showing your work before the gallery offers you a one man or two man show.

The gallery will have periodic shows often linked to seasons or festivals.

They will often operate largely as picture shops with a mixed stock of prints and originals.

They most likely offer a framing service, which earns them more money than the art shows.

You should approach the gallery only after doing a bit of homework.

Start by visiting if possible without revealing that you are an artist trying to exhibit with them. See how they perform. Watch the gallery staff as they sell and deal with other browsing visitors. Ask to see something else by one of the artists already on show and see if the gallery has a stock of work in reserve as well as the stock on display. You are justified in this sneaky anonymous approach because you may be saving yourself and the gallery a lot of time by discovering that the gallery is wrong for you, or that you are wrong for the gallery.

Step two is to find out as much as possible about the gallery before you make open contact. Visit the gallery website and look for the 'about us' button. Gather the name and details of the person who makes the buying and exhibiting decisions. Ask around especially ask other artists who are exhibited if you can find where to contact them.

Then, stage three, make an approach where you will ask for an appointment to show them some of your work. They should be willing to see your work, especially if you have a well-prepared brochure, so send them your brochure first and follow up with a phone call.

Stage four, the appointment. Be on time. Have a small selection of your best work with you. Have an idea of your prices but make it very plain that you would greatly value the advice of the gallery professional. So listen more than talk.

This is what might happen.

The gallery owner will not like your work.

So make sure that you get something positive from the meeting by asking what he/she thinks you could do to make it better. Ask if the gallery owner can put you in touch with another gallery where your work would be more suitable. Thank the gallery owner for the time and advice that you have been given.

> ### GOLDEN RULE NUMBER 10: BE POSITIVE AND KEEP YOUR CHIN UP.
>
> You must reckon on the inevitable fact that you will get rejected many times before you get accepted. So, no worry, you have just got another rejection out of the way, and you are a little bit closer to getting your next big break.

The gallery owner likes your work but cannot use it in the gallery.

You could repeat the responses above, plus ask for a chance to keep in touch so that when you have other work available you can show it to them.

The gallery likes your work and wants to try it out.

The gallery will probably ask for some work on sale or return, or on consignment, to show in the gallery out of exhibition time. You are unlikely to be offered space in a show without the gallery dipping a toe in the water first. So snap up this chance and agree to lend the gallery a couple of pieces for a month. However, take with you a piece of paper when you deliver the pictures which sets out in simple terms exactly what you are letting them have and what the terms are. Get it signed. Go back at the end of the agreed term, a month would be a fair start, and either collect the pictures, or renegotiate to leave them for a bit longer, or send an invoice, or collect the money.

<u>Don't forget about the pictures, but don't hassle the gallery before the month is up.</u>

So where is the bit about the gallery liking your work and wanting to buy it straight away?

Well it doesn't happen, so I didn't put it in. A gallery will not buy from you until it knows that it can sell your work. They will know that they cannot always be sure of their own taste. What they like might not be what sells. Remember nasty shock no. 4 in Chapter 5?

A two or three man show in a commercial gallery.

A commercial art gallery will probably offer you a chance to participate in a special two, three or more artist show if the sales from the general part of the shop have been successful.

Not all commercial galleries are suitable for this kind of show. Galleries that sell mainly to a passing and ever-changing audience like those in tourist localities or the seaside, will not have so much interest in this kind of special show.

But if the gallery is in a town or city with a repeat audience, and a nurtured mailing list, then this is the kind of exhibition that can really put you on the map. The gallery will give you plenty of notice. Maybe even a couple of years notice! This is because the gallery will have a programme of exhibitions and will be promoting the work with a mail out and specially printed invitations to a private view etc..

A one-man show in a commercial gallery.

If the gallery group show worked well, and the gallery sees a good chance of collectors buying your work again, then you could get a one-man show. The gallery will be putting a lot of faith in you if it offers you a show like this. They will be willing to risk a lot of effort and money. You will be given plenty of notice and help by the gallery about what to paint, how to prepare the work, and what to expect. So you will only get an offer like this if the gallery is absolutely sure that you are loyal, and trustworthy, and professional.

A one-man show in a prestigious public institution or museum.

The top of the prestige ladder is a one-man show in a national public gallery or similar. You will be approached, or your gallery agent will be approached, and the event will be planned ages in advance. Unfortunately it usually happens only after you are dead. Hey ho!

But your own local town might give you a show along these lines if you become well known during your lifetime, just because they are proud of you.

Chapter Six.....Conclusion

This chapter is titled 'Showing Off'. This is what you do if you are an artist.

You are bound to come a cropper every now and then, so there was another Golden Rule...Be positive and keep your chin up.

That makes ten Golden Rules so far.

GOLDEN RULE No 1:   **INVEST AND BELIEVE IN YOURSELF.**

GOLDEN RULE No 2:   **KEEP RECORDS.**

GOLDEN RULE No 3:   **AIM FOR QUALITY.**

GOLDEN RULE No 4:   **BE BUSINESSLIKE.**

GOLDEN RULE No 5:   **SEEK AND LISTEN TO EXPERT ADVICE.**

GOLDEN RULE No 6:   **FOCUS YOUR EFFORT.**

GOLDEN RULE No 7:   **JOIN UP, MEET PEOPLE, NETWORK.**

GOLDEN RULE No 8:   **BE PREPARED, TURN UP.**

GOLDEN RULE No 9:   **DON'T EXPECT FAIRY GODMOTHERS.**

GOLDEN RULE No 10:   **BE POSITIVE AND KEEP YOUR CHIN UP.**

GOLDEN RULE No 11:   **?**

GOLDEN RULE No 12:   **?**

CHAPTER SEVEN: Selling

In which we discuss selling your work, and taking the money.

In this chapter we shall look at your techniques for selling and taking the money. What is so difficult about that?

You might be a natural sales person, who will find some of this very basic, but quite likely you are an artist with little previous sales experience and you could make some costly mistakes. These mistakes might be the difference between survival as an artist and failure.

Credit card sales

You will need to take credit card payments from your customers. Go to your bank and set up a merchant services account to enable you to take visa and MasterCard. Go to American Express to take Amex cards if you have any ambition to sell on the internet or in the USA.

The percentage commission rates will vary depending on your projected turnover, type of sales [telephone, direct or internet], delay before getting paid, and the kind of terminal you use to contact the card service for authorisation. If you belong to a trade organisation you will probably find that you can get good deals through them.

If you tell the service provider that you expect to sell mostly over the telephone or from your website then you may be asked to pay a higher charge because the card holder will not be present to sign the card in front of you. So the percentage of fraudulent buyers who give you a stolen or made up card number is higher. Banks know this and will charge accordingly.

Beware that you don't sign up for something with a high commission charge and a long-term contract until you know what your sales methods are likely to be.

The main advantages to you of a credit card facility are that you get paid long before the customer settles the bill with the card company, and you will be able to sell to impulse buyers.

Post dated cheques

You can get by, before you set up a merchant account to take credit cards, by accepting post dated cheques from keen buyers who haven't got all the money at the time that they wish to buy. Before the advent of credit cards this was the only sensible way to allow a customer to take possession of your picture before payment in full.

You will ask the customer for the total amount paid in instalments in several cheques dated over future months. You will present each of these cheques as the date becomes due. The risk is usually quite small that you will get a bouncing cheque, but it is a good idea to remind a customer who buys with post dated cheques when another cheque is due for presentation to your bank.

Don't phone to remind them because that way you are inviting the customer to ask you to wait another couple of weeks. Just send them a note or email to say that the cheque will be going in at the due date and how much that is, because they may have forgotten.

The benefits to your customer, by taking credit cards or post dated cheques, are that they can spread their payments over several weeks or months to suit their budget. And you will be able to sell the collector much more by offering this service, and a handful of post dated cheques will give you an income flow so that you can see where your next meal is coming from.

Lay away schemes

An alternative to the get the picture now and pay later schemes is a pay by instalments scheme where you let the client take the goods only after the bill has been paid in full. Your risk is much lower and some collectors do not like any sort of credit hanging over them.

Offering this alternative is a good idea, but you have to store the picture while you wait for full payment. You will need to have cast iron record keeping because there is nothing so irate as a collector who comes to collect their picture who is told that here is still yet another payment to be made. Are you sure that they didn't pay an instalment last January?

Pro-forma Invoices

A pro-forma invoice is one where you as the seller agree an order with your customer. You send the customer a **pro-forma** invoice for the value of the goods. You deliver the goods only after you have been paid. This is common practice where you are dealing with new trade customers. Established trade customers will expect an ordinary invoice and will usually pay 30 days after the date of invoice and after receiving the goods.

Renting

Another scheme is to rent the picture to your buyer until the agreed price is paid in full. This means that you do not have to store the picture while retaining legal title to it until you exchange ownership in exchange for final payment. Again good record keeping and a good contract are vital.

Corporate buyers might be more amenable to this than private buyers because many offices rent all their fixtures and fittings such as pictures, water coolers, flowers etc. to avoid capital outlay.

Barter

You might consider bartering your art object for some other goods or service. I swapped one of my small early paintings for a tape recorder and another for a set of tables and chairs that we still use forty years later. Artists are often able to make such deals, and you could make the opening suggestion if your selling attempt comes up against a willing buyer without spare cash. If you don't know how to open the discussion start by asking what the interested buyer does for a living to see if there is a swap possibility available. You could find that once they know that you are open to bartering they will offer all sorts of goodies that you would want in exchange.

Exchange.

A way to encourage a buyer who is hesitant for one reason or another is to offer to exchange back the artwork any time in the future. You can offer to change the piece for another of the same value or put the purchase price towards another of increased value.

It is not necessary to offer the buyer his or her money back. You may not be able to afford that at the time. But a straight exchange for a different piece would not cost you anything.

You must keep those records to know exactly how much the customer can have as credit if they exchange. Only accept a piece in exchange if it is undamaged and in the same condition that you sold it. Make this clear when you offer the exchange option. Exchanging can make the difference between a sale and a refusal.

SOR.

Many galleries will not buy work from artists. They only work on Sale or Return, also called 'on consignment'. There are some legal differences between the two terms but generally they work the same for you. Basically the gallery will take your work and display it for sale. The work belongs to you. You have 'retained title to the work'. The gallery will add their mark up to your price, or agree with you what the selling price should be and take a commission from the sale proceeds. The gallery will collect the money and then you will be expected to invoice the gallery for your amount.

The thing to watch here is that quite a few galleries will take your work and sell it and then wait for you to ask for it back before telling you that it has been sold. That way the gallery hangs on to all the money for as long as possible. Some artists even forget where and what they have out on SOR. KEEP RECORDS!

Another snag is that the gallery may exhibit your work for a short while and then put it away in store without any real chance of being sold. So keep in touch with the gallery and get the work back if it is not sold pretty quickly. [I wish I had always taken my own advice here.]

Encourage collectors.

Collectors are probably your best chance of discovering an 80/20 split. Previous buyers will be much more likely to buy from you than anyone else. Keep records and keep in touch. Send out newsletters and make special offers to your ever-growing list of collectors. You could try discounts but this may not be a good idea. You could offer pre-publication reservations of artist's proofs for a new print edition. You could offer private view invitations with wine and nibbles to help them enjoy themselves. You could offer a chance to sponsor an exhibition or auction for charity.

Direct selling

Direct selling to the end user/collector has a big advantage over selling into the picture trade. Specifically the price to you is better because you are not paying a middleman. So explore a variety of ways to sell directly if you can possibly do it. But of course you will have to do the selling. So learn some basic selling techniques.

Remember the basics,

1. **Turn up**

2. **Get their attention**

3. **Present your USP [unique selling point]**

4. **Inform**

5. **Listen**

6. **Watch for buying signals**

7. **Close**

8. **Get out**

If you have any problems with any of this then find out more by internet research, or take a short course, or read a book. Here are some notes that might help.

Turning up

Turning up or getting together with your prospective customer is 80% of the task. I think it was Woody Allen who when asked for the secret of his success as an actor answered 'turning up'. This is also important for artist sales person to realise because it means that you have to find your prospect, make an appointment, get on your bike, open your studio, advertise, or what ever it takes. Somehow or the other you must first show your art to the customer. So many sales people fail because they fail to get their product in front of customers. You have got to find a way that will put you and the art and the prospective customer together.

Find your target niche, make contact, prepare, and turn up.

Getting attention

Getting attention is crucial. Especially in a show where there is a lot of competition, or in someone's house while the television is on, or in your studio when the customer is distracted by your décor, or anywhere when their friend wants to tell them about a wonderful purchase they made while on holiday last year. Watch for the signs and attract the customer's attention as much as possible. You can lose many sales at this stage after all your hard work getting the art in front of them.

Present your USP [unique selling point].

Your USP is the special something that will set you apart from any competition. It might be that you were first, or best, or have won an award. It might be that your art is bigger, brighter, or bolder. It might be that the subject is about something unique, or you the artist have some special technique. Anything, which makes your art different and special, is useful. Work it out for yourself and then present your USP to the prospect. They must be able to say to themselves that this is the special reason for buying from you and not from someone else. Don't completely rely on the art to sell itself.

Inform

Inform the prospective customer about everything that they need to know in order to get the sale. Be prepared to explain painting or printing methods, and framing costs, and care requirements. Have this information ready, and answer all queries quickly and truthfully. Don't pretend to know the answer to anything that you don't know, better to admit that you have been asked an interesting question and you will find out and let them know later. Get back to the sale process and remember to tell them the answer after you find out.

Listen

Listen to the prospect. You will get further and get a sale quicker if you encourage them to tell you why the picture appeals to them. So ask, and then listen. You can talk yourself out of a sale just by not allowing them to buy, because you are so busy telling them all about you and your art. You could find out from them what they want, where it is going to hang, how much they can spend, what they like, how it will be framed, how they found you, etc.. You have so much to find out, and they will probably love to tell you because you are showing interest in them.

Watch for buying signals.

Oh this is tricky! But it is very important if you can get it right. They might ask you about payment, or delivery, or something that shows that they are willing to buy if you answer the next question right. So answer the question and watch for the signal that tells you that you have said the right thing....THEN POUNCE. I don't mean pounce in an obvious way, just smile and make the little move that will encourage them to follow your lead into the next phase. There comes a time when you will be able to assume a sale without putting the prospect into the position of having to assert their intention. Get to know these signals and watch for them.

Close.

The simplest way to close the sale is to start to write down something on your order pad. Ask for the clients name or address. Make a note of the details of the sale on a special bit of paper. You can give lots of smiles, and get into the process of taking the order, which you have obviously done many times before. This will reassure the customer and they will go along with your process, which will end up with the payment and post sale details such as delivery or collection dates.

Get out.

Then get out of the situation in a dignified and comfortable manner. The temptation might be to linger and talk more. After all you have just made friends with the new customer. That is good but keep it short. You have set up a successful selling situation haven't you, so you should be looking for the next sale now that you know that you have a formula. You want to be free to attend to the next customer or find the next prospect, so thank the buyer for their interest and go, or let them go.

Chapter Seven ..... conclusion

Some one said that selling is a lot like fishing.

You must fish in a pond where there are fish. You cannot catch fish in an empty lake or river. You must get your art in front of people who buy art. You will not sell your art to people that do not buy art or if they don't know about it. You can sell your art to people that like it as long as you have got them to see it.

You must use bait that the fish like. You will not sell your art to people who do not like your art, or if it is the wrong art. You must have the right sales tools in order to be able to sell your art. Your sales tools include knowledge of selling techniques and alternatives.

You must use the right hook. You can sell your art if you present it well, if you sell it well and if you strike at the right time. You must offer your art and provide a reason to act now.

That makes ten Golden Rules so far.

GOLDEN RULE No 1: **INVEST AND BELIEVE IN YOURSELF.**

GOLDEN RULE No 2: **KEEP RECORDS.**

GOLDEN RULE No 3: **AIM FOR QUALITY.**

GOLDEN RULE No 4: **BE BUSINESSLIKE.**

GOLDEN RULE No 5: **SEEK AND LISTEN TO EXPERT ADVICE.**

GOLDEN RULE No 6: **FOCUS YOUR EFFORT.**

GOLDEN RULE No 7: **JOIN UP, MEET PEOPLE, NETWORK.**

GOLDEN RULE No 8: **BE PREPARED, TURN UP.**

GOLDEN RULE No 9: **DON'T EXPECT A FAIRY GODMOTHER.**

GOLDEN RULE No 10: **BE POSITIVE AND KEEP YOUR CHIN UP.**

GOLDEN RULE No 11: **?**

GOLDEN RULE No 12: **?**

CHAPTER EIGHT: Playing to the gallery

More about your relationship with galleries and dealers.

Myths about galleries

- Galleries make or break artists
- You must be represented by a gallery to be a real artist
- Galleries pay artists on time
- Gallery owners are good business people
- Gallery owners are organised

Cottage industry.

Here in the UK the gallery system has been described as 'the last cottage industry'. The typical British town has a handful of small art galleries typically ranging from an established long term traditional gallery employing three or four staff selling original paintings and limited edition prints with picture framing and sculpture, ceramics and cards as extra products. At the other end of the scale are small artist owned back street shops, or even homes selling crafts and art materials, and doing picture framing and cards as well as the artists own work, with some extra artists to add variety. The former will probably have been a family enterprise that has survived a few decades, and the latter will be quite new with the artist and spouse running the shop.

What there is not is a chain of art galleries like there is a chain of chemists, shoe shops, clothes retailers or furniture stores. The nearest that there has been to the chain was the franchised picture framer, although most of these have now become independent. Some picture framers that were franchise holders also sell pictures. Most of them are now virtually the same as independent galleries.

Another group is a poster shop chain selling posters and pre-framed open edition art and cards, characterised by no originals and no exhibitions.

There are a very few art gallery groups with a gallery having a second or third outlet as well as the main one. The biggest group has six galleries.

Department store galleries

There are some department store art galleries that are run by the department store in house. These represent the biggest central buying group of retailers in the UK. Examples at the moment include the John Lewis Partnership.

But beware because many other department stores franchise out the space to independent retailers who run the art gallery inside the store. They buy and sell just like a high street gallery. Some are linked in partnership contracts to major publishing companies which in effect means that you will not be able to sell to them without a contract with that publisher.

In Japan the department store is a much bigger influence on the art retailer. Here is a reprint of my article written for the UK art trade press after a trip to Japan in 2003.

Big in Japan

"The average height of the Japanese is 159 cm. [I am 180 cm., or just over 5'10" in old money]. So by invitation and feeling big with a height advantage of 21 cm., I recently visited and whizzed round Japan on a thousand mile, whirlwind, handshake, photo-shoot, publicity tour, visiting ten art galleries that were holding simultaneous exhibitions of my work. I was treated with the status of visiting royalty, which was flattering, exciting, profitable, and fun. I also learned something about the Japanese way of art-business.

The system is different over there. Art galleries are largely situated in huge department stores, which are often linked directly to train and tube stations by a warren of wide subterranean walkways. From train to gallery can be a mind numbing experience and it is easy to get disorientated and lost because the passages are jostling with people, shops, stalls, and restaurants, with complex lift and escalator connections The galleries open at department store times, usually 10 am to 8 pm seven days a week. The gallery proprietor depends on the department store to supply premises, heating, lighting and a steady flow of the right customers. In exchange the department store insist on a very high standard of service for the customer. Retail galleries pay for space in the department stores with a percentage of turnover.

The art gallery chain that sells my work has twelve retail outlets, and a sister company supplying many others with picture frames. Altogether they have a workforce of around 250 and even supply housing for key employees in company owned apartment blocks. Personnel are likely to stay with the same company for many years, with wages in Japan a little higher than UK.

My dealer buys my work unframed in the UK and frames to a very high standard in Japan. Everything is behind glass, even originals on canvas. Retail prices are a little more that UK prices, probably largely due to shipping and promotional costs. The customer is supplied with a finished and beautifully presented product by highly trained and uniformed sales teams.

In the UK a gallery might promote an artist with a private view occasion lubricated with wine and nibbles. In Japan the department store venue restricts the gallery dealer to a different sort of promotion, a favourite being the personal appearance by an artist rather akin to an authors book-signing event put on by literary publishing houses. My events were well publicised and many customers had booked appointments to meet me and ask questions about the work. Typically meetings started with bowing, shaking hands and a photo-shoot. Many collectors bought gifts. They always wanted their purchase to be signed on the back of the picture, often requiring a message and date linking the sale to an event such as birthdays or moving house. Thus I was able to find out what and why they liked about my pictures directly from the collector. I was able to present each customer with a photograph memento of our meeting in a presentation folder at the end of every interview.

Socialising after work is the norm. On my first evening I met with local staff for a welcome dinner. We knelt on the floor and ate with chopsticks in a room with paper walls and sliding doors. A woman wearing a kimono served our food. The laughing and friendly greeting from my hosts was infectious. I tried everything on the table even though much of the first meal was strange and unknown. I don't think it is connected, but on that first night there was a local earthquake measuring 3.5 on the Richter scale. It wobbled the bed and shook the curtains. My hotel room was on the 19th floor and the building swayed a little. It put the wind up me, but these tremors are common enough with maybe one or two a month.

One evening we dined with the 'master printer' who has previously printed my, and many other artists, silk-screens and litho in Japan. The Japanese giclee technology that has revolutionised the Western publishing scene was initially treated with great suspicion in their home country. Cultural habits and aesthetic idiosyncrasies were well entrenched and harder to overcome. I was introduced to the concept of, 'aesthetic imperfection', where craft and art conspire to make deliberately flawed artwork to accentuate the beauty of non-mechanical production. However, the 'master printer' is just taking delivery of his first giclee machine. Giclee resistance is crumbling.

On journeys within cities everybody seems to use the train or tube. These are crowded day and night and usually entailed standing for an hour or so to get from one venue to another. Electronic displays and voice messages are often in Japanese and English. Passengers queue between marked lines on the platform waiting for the next train.

Between major cities we travelled on 'Shinkansen' or bullet trains. These departed on the main line between Tokyo and Kyoto, Kobe, and Osaka every 15 mins., exactly on time. Journey duration in clean roomy comfort at 168 mph from the new capital Tokyo, to the ancient capital Kyoto, was 2hr 35mins. A gentle recorded voice greets passengers in English and asks that all mobile phones be set to silent mode. [Now that IS a GOOD IDEA]. There was a buffet and trolley service for refreshments. All train personnel entering the carriage bowed in the connecting doorway and bowed again before leaving. We whizzed through endless suburbs that stretched for hundreds of miles. About 80% of Japans 120 million people live on the coastal plain on the south side of the main island Honshu. The little bits of agriculture viewed from the speeding train showed small clean tidy arable fields with no livestock visible anywhere at all.

The market for Western art is not so huge as a population of 120 million affluent middle-class people would suppose. Small houses, small rooms and sliding doors limit wall space. Nevertheless my own London and New York scenes are doing well, as are Cornish harbour and Mediterranean scenes. Interestingly, advice given by dealers in Japan to erstwhile Japanese abstract artists is 'go to Paris, London or America because you won't succeed in Japan'.

The 'come-away-with' impression is of a safe, clean, punctual, busy, crowded, island country full of prosperous and hospitable people. They relish modern technological invention with the latest mobile camera/internet phones but the electricity supply cables are all in great tangles of wires up poles on every street. Eating establishments' show their menus with realistic plastic replica meals to make choice easy, supply diners with warm flannels and cold water, yet do not have lap protecting napkins for the clumsy western chopstick user. They eat healthy nutritious food, work in modern and startling architectural conditions, yet have tiny homes, no gardens, and stand for an hour and a half to and from work every day. They enjoy eating while sitting cross-legged or kneeling in excruciating pain, yet have exquisitely warm heated toilet seats. The art collector is treated to fantastic personal attention and the art is beautifully presented, but there is less choice available than in the UK.

My hosts were very efficient and generous, and the collectors that I met were overwhelmingly complimentary. A remark that took me by *surprise the first time, and thrilled me by the number of times it was repeated, was; "You so cute. You look like gentleman. You look like Sean Connery, he my most handsome man in the world."*

The secret fellahs is to have grey stubble, an old felt hat, and be average UK height!"

Partnership contracts.

In recent years two of the major art publishing houses in the UK have established a partnership arrangement with some galleries. These 'partners' have accepted funds and marketing help from the publisher in exchange for an exclusivity deal that concentrates them on selling work published from the single publishing source. Some one hundred or so galleries up and down the country are tied up in these schemes.

These galleries tend to look the same and be limited in the stock available from the big publishers. Their contracts oblige them to buy from the publisher so that when the publisher launches a new edition from an artist the edition is almost instantly 'sold out' because the whole edition has been forced upon the 'partners'.

This gallery/publisher relationship has been described as 'the dark side' of the industry because it effectively stifles much of the competition.

Independents.

The remaining galleries are typically run by independent family members, and are often set up by an artist, craftsman, or picture framer. The start up funds probably came from a redundancy, retirement, or down sizing in the property market.

The entrepreneur gallery owner borrows more funds to take on a lease, kit out a gallery with flooring, lighting, framing equipment, counters, browsers and coffee machine, and then begs borrows or makes the produce to sell in it.

Operating costs, heat, light, rent, rates or council tax, telephone, insurance, wages for part time staff make the business viability very precarious.

So most of the thousand or so galleries in the UK are independents, and have no central command, pool of funds, or even a buying policy.

The bottom line is this…**there is nothing left in the kitty, for most of the galleries in the UK, to spend on your pictures.**

The gallery owner therefore resorts to offering to display your goods on sale or return, whilst making his/her living by doing picture framing.

The exceptions are there of course. Good gallery businesses can be found where the gallery is able to invest in stock from good selling artists because they have a history of good sound business practice and have made profits to reinvest. Some of these are still independent and have resisted 'the dark side'. Some of these even put pictures before framing as their focal point. If you know one, make friends with them quickly.

First division 'Fine Art' galleries

The elite sector of the art retail business can be found in the major cities, especially London. These galleries are selling big artist names at big prices. A gaggle of them exist in Bond Street London. You can recognise them because they do not have a big picture framing display, extra ceramic display shelves, greetings cards, or poster browsers. Realistically as an artist you have no chance of getting into one of these. Here is why.

The market in super fine investment art, the kind of art sold in Bond Street, has a special, crucial and unique feature. This is the fact that at the very top of the market tree are the national collections. Every civilised country in the world has a national gallery, which holds the nation's treasures specialising of course in the nation's own artists. National art collections and institutional art collections usually have a policy that encourages them to spend public or institutional money to buy the next important artists work before it gets too expensive to afford.

The weird distorting factor about these collections is that once a picture goes into this area it stays there never to be sold again. There is a one-way exit through which certain art goes and never reappears. The national collections hold on to their art with iron grips.

The reason is that while an artist is alive, the importance of his/her total work is unknowable, either in quantity or quality. Only history can tell who is or was important in art. It might take fifty or so years after an artist death by which time all work will be spoken for.

The national gallery curator will be on a limited budget and must collect while they can afford the work so they acquire work while artists are alive and comparably cheap. Because as soon as an artist is dead the potential value and cost goes up as dealers bid to acquire work in case the art world sees this artist as significant. No one in this game wants to be left without an example of the favoured artist in the national collection.

In Bond Street and elsewhere the gallery trade is affected by the potential super rise in value if an artist becomes a big name and needs to be acquired by the national collections. There are shoals of investment sharks collecting artists' work if the artist smells of future importance.

There are some astute buyers who will look through art students degree shows and buy up pieces with the idea that they will clean up as soon as a top gallery or dealer/collector, like Charles Saatchi, takes up the artist.

And of course there is Saatchi himself. Probably he will have approached a likely young art student before he/she even leaves the Royal College or other major institution. In the USA there are many such investment buyers circling like sharks around a dying whale calf.

They want the artist to be taken up by a good gallery, and put under a tight contract, which will control the supply of art and ensure that the market remains scarce. They also want the artist to make something individual and different.

Feeding frenzy.

Why can't I get into this feeding frenzy you ask.

Because the likely artists are spotted while still at one of the major prestigious art colleges like the Royal College in London. They are usually under contract to a major international dealer before they leave college. They will be nurtured and mentored and their production will be controlled from the very beginning of their artistic careers. It is crucial to the investment value of their work that all of their production is catalogued and that they do not over produce.

If you are reading this book it probably means that it did not happen to you. It didn't happen to me either.

Occasionally a good artist can confound this gallery system and be recognised as a potential important artist late in his/her life. Such an artist was Lowry who was a council rent collector for his working life but became a big collectable name after he retired.

But here in this book we do not rely on fairy godmothers or very lucky breaks. It is possible to make a good living as an artist without coming into contact with the Bond Street gallery crowd.

And in the USA.

I can recommend that you download an article by Brooks Jensen about the Gallery System for photographers in the USA. The analysis is good and the problems are the same. See www.lenswork.com

Chapter Eight... conclusion

This chapter is titled 'Playing to the gallery', more about relationships with galleries and dealers.

The UK gallery system is changing in the face of new developments to the traditional power base of fine art publishers.

Some publishers are moving strongly into a retail position.

Independent artists must keep an eye on these changes and use their nimble low cost advantage to their best ability.

GOLDEN RULE No 1: **INVEST AND BELIEVE IN YOURSELF.**

GOLDEN RULE No 2: **KEEP RECORDS.**

GOLDEN RULE No 3: **AIM FOR QUALITY.**

GOLDEN RULE No 4: **BE BUSINESSLIKE.**

GOLDEN RULE No 5: **SEEK AND LISTEN TO EXPERT ADVICE.**

GOLDEN RULE No 6: **FOCUS YOUR EFFORT.**

GOLDEN RULE No 7: **JOIN UP, MEET PEOPLE, NETWORK.**

GOLDEN RULE No 8: **BE PREPARED, TURN UP.**

GOLDEN RULE No 9: **DON'T EXPECT A FAIRY GODMOTHER**

GOLDEN RULE No 10: **BE POSITIVE AND KEEP YOUR CHIN UP.**

GOLDEN RULE No 11: **?**

GOLDEN RULE No 12: **?**

CHAPTER NINE: One day my prints will come

Going into print, and getting famous:
the four important issues

A bit of history.

Etching appeared as decoration on Italian armour in the 14th century.

Probably some one noticed that if you made the incised surface of a decorated breastplate dirty, then pressed something soft against it, you had a reverse print of the etched image on the soft surface.

The first block prints were cut into metal using techniques borrowed from armour decoration.

The language for techniques and tools still used in etching and engraving is based on the Italian or French terms used in armour decoration, e.g. intaglio, *roulette*, mattoir.

Breughel and contemporaries used prints to market work at a cheaper price than original paintings. The earliest woodcuts date from the end of the 14th century, the first dated etching is from 1513. The first lithograph in 1798. The first Iris giclee print in 1990.

[Information from New York Society of Etchers.]

ISSUE NUMBER ONE

Original prints or reproductions, or neither!

Once upon a time life was very simple. There were two easily distinguishable kinds of prints.

- **Reproductions** The most common kind of prints were usually reproductions done on huge litho presses, and mass-produced, with little or no long-term value except as wall decoration.

- **Original prints** Were done by hand, by the artist or craftsman using traditional techniques like etching or woodblock, usually one by one, usually in a very small edition, and were not reproductions of another artwork.

Traditional printing methods for original prints were,

- Hand pulled lithography
- Silkscreen (aka serigraphy)
- Etching
- Lino cut
- Wood block
- Engraving

The distinction continues today, except that the water got a lot muddier at the end of the 20th century, with the advent of giclee printing.

Giclee prints [see below] can be stunning in quality. But they are digitally controlled by computers and may not be accepted as hand produced. The purists, and the Luddites, are unwilling, or slow, to accept digital printing into the 'original print' category.

ISSUE NUMBER TWO

Limited editions or Open editions, or neither!

Limited editions, a bit more history.

Fifty odd years ago the tax system in the UK included a purchase tax where the retailer had to add a tax at point of sale. The tax rate varied and luxury items were taxed very highly. 25% tax rate on luxury goods was typical. Decorative items were seen as luxury goods.

However original art was free of tax. Prints posed a dilemma for the governing authorities. Were they art and tax free, or were they luxury items and subject to 25% tax. The solution was simple. Prints designated as 'limited editions' with a maximum of 75 prints in the edition were classified as 'original art' and were tax-free. Open editions with no restriction on the total amount produced and sold were taxed heavily.

The British art market therefore learned to prize 'limited editions' much higher than 'open editions'.

Purchase tax was abolished when Value Added Tax [VAT] was introduced at the time of Britain applying to join the Common Market where VAT was a required tax. But the legacy continues, and 'limited editions' are still prized as potential collectables, whilst 'open editions' or reproductions are not, except in rare circumstances. Some reproductions do have a perceived value in investment terms, if the artist is particularly well known and the prints are rare, but usually the dealers are only interested in original prints sold in limited editions.

In the rest of the English-speaking world a 'limited edition' has similar status to the UK, although the accepted standards are much stricter in the UK than anywhere else in the world.

It is interesting to note that in the rest of Europe 'limited editions' are not as highly thought of as here in the UK.

In the USA it seems to be more readily accepted that a publisher can produce a 'limited edition' and when it is sold out they can subsequently produce an open edition using the same image.

The Fine Art Trade Guild standard for a limited edition says that the image must not be used in any other edition worldwide forever except for promotional purposes such as in a brochure or in a book.

Open edition/Poster

There is a huge market for prints all over the world. The major publishers of open edition posters do not usually deal in limited editions as well. Retail prices, and hence profit margins, on posters are smaller than limited editions, but posters sell in huge quantities to a much wider audience.

Open editions are printed in much greater volume and so the printing method is usually four-colour lithography. That is the kind of print process that prints magazines and advertising leaflets. Art prints are usually on quite good paper and long-lasting non-fading inks might be used, [if the buyer is lucky].

Most of the best selling open editions are reproductions of paintings or photographs. It is unusual to find a hand signed open edition, and individual print numbering is very unusual indeed.

ISSUE NUMBER THREE

Different types of print

TRADITIONAL PRINTMAKING

Intaglio Printing – Prepared by Andy P. Hoogenboom

Intaglio printing is produced by various methods, all of which involve lines, grooves, and marks engraved or etched into metal plates and printed onto paper using a hand press. The first printing is known as a proof. The artist can rework the plate and take further "states' until the final impression is achieved.

While there are various methods, among the most commonly practiced are: Etching; Aquatint; Dry point; Mezzotint; and Engraving.

Etching

Etching refers to an image making process using acids that bite into metal. A plate (usually copper or zinc) is coated with a wax-based acid-resistant ground. The design is then drawn, scraped, or pressed into the ground to expose predetermined areas of the metal. The plate is then submerged in acid that "bites" into the areas where the metal is exposed. The plate is removed when the desired depth of "bite" is achieved.

Aquatint

Aquatint refers to a print made by using a porous ground of powdered rosin dusted evenly on a metal plate that is then fused to the surface with heat. Tonality is achieved by different periods of immersion in acid (usually Ferric Chloride) that bites tiny dots in to the metal plate through the pores of the rosin. The density of the dots determines the effect because these dots hold varying amounts of ink during the printing process. Tone can be further manipulated by using a scraper or burnisher on the plate. Many print makers, past and present, combine etching and aquatint.

Dry point

Dry point images are made by drawing, cross-hatching, scratching, and gouging directly into a metal plate, using a needle made from hard steel or diamond point (hence "point"). No acid is used in this process, hence the term "dry". Some prints are made using the dry point technique alone but it is often used in conjunction with other intaglio printing techniques.

Mezzotint

Mezzotints can be identified by their rich, often dark, tonal surfaces. These surfaces are created by roughing-up the surface of a metal plate with a multi-needled tool. The tool is rocked in many directions in order to impress the entire surface of the plate with tiny "pits" (indentations). The image is created by burnishing or scraping the surface to various depths, thus creating a variety of tones -- from dense black, through quarter and half tones, to white.

Engraving

Engraving is a process whereby lines and grooves are cut into a metal plate with a "burin" (a triangular, knife-like tool). Cutting is always done in one direction; the plate itself is swivelled to achieve new angles and directions. This method offers a great deal of control to the printmaker. The differing depths of line – from fine line to deep groove – accounts for marks that range from delicate to dramatic.

Thanks to Andy Hoogenboom in New York for the preceding section on intaglio printing.

Etching, Engraving, Mezzotint, Aquatint, Drypoint.

Etching, engraving and woodblock printing are very traditional processes with skilled crafts-persons needed to make the plates or blocks. Each print is printed one at a time, usually in one colour only. Adding colour can be done but involves a new plate or block for each colour unless each print is coloured using watercolour by hand. The print runs are very often very low, often only 10 or 20 prints in the edition.

An engraver, etcher etc. cuts an image into the metal of a plate, then inks the whole plate, then wipes the ink off the raised surface.

Damp paper and the plate are run through a press. The paper is pressed very firmly against the plate and the ink that is held in the incised surface and is transferred to the paper.

As you can see there are characteristics of an intaglio-processed print,

- The process prints one colour at a time.
- The paper is in direct contact with the plate.
- The printed image is a reverse mirror image of the plate.
- The pressure of printing may indent the paper at the edges of the print.
- The surface of the print image does not print.
- The printed image reflects the cut away portion of the plate.

Lino cut, Wood block

These prints are usually made by cutting into a surface of the 'block' to make the white space, and inking the raised surface. This is followed by pressing the inked lino/wood-block onto the paper.

Lino cut uses [wait for it] lino, and a wood block uses [yawn] wood. The process can also be called cameo or relief printing.

As you can see there are characteristics of a cameo or relief processed print,

- The process prints one colour at a time.
- The paper is in direct contact with the plate/lino/wood.
- The printed image is a reverse mirror image of the plate/lino/wood.
- Oil or water based inks can be used.
- Can be done with very little equipment enabling home production.

Lithography

Litho is Greek for stone. The first lithographs used stone slabs but nowadays the industry normally uses metal or plastic plates.

The process involves using the natural resistance of water and oil. An image is created onto a plate or stone slab using a greasy substance.

The greasy marks are hardened and strengthened, and then a film of water is wiped across the surface of the whole plate/stone. Ink is then rolled across the surface and sticks to the greasy marks but is resisted by the water on the non-greasy areas.

A paper is then laid onto the plate, or rolled against the plate, and the ink is thus transferred to the paper from the plate.

The process can be repeated many times and a series of 'prints' can be pulled.

As you can see there are characteristics of a hand pulled litho;

- The process prints one colour at a time.
- The paper is in direct contact with the plate.
- The printed image is a reverse mirror image of the image on the plate
- Oil based inks are used.

For a hand-pulled litho the image can be made up from many plates with a new plate for each colour and utilising any colour that the artist chooses. The process is slow, requiring re-inking the plate by hand after each print is pulled. There are hand presses where the image is transferred from the plate onto a roller and then onto the paper thus keeping the image positive.

A cheaper alternative is the four-colour litho process. This process is a lot more mechanised, especially when used commercially for magazines etc.. It utilises four colours, cyan, magenta, yellow and black, CMYK.

The main difference is that the plates are made using an electro-photo-mechanical process, which reproduces an image into four dot screens where the dot size increases apparent density of colour. The resulting four colour plates can be combined to reproduce most of the colours in the visible spectrum, but not all. The huge presses involved in mass production litho printing print at tremendous speed.

This is the process used by many poster publishers, and chosen for cheaper open editions. Before giclee, big publishers of limited editions used litho. The process prints all the colours at once, and at great speed. But again the whole edition has to be printed in one go. The cost of printing on a half million pound printer means that only publishing houses are able to afford it. A humble artist could easily be asked for £5000 up front to print an edition. Then he/she has the problem of storage and distribution. It is very unlikely that any artist can afford to publish a portfolio of say 24 images showing his/her work.

As you can see there are characteristics of a four-colour mechanised litho,

- The process prints all four colours at once.
- The paper is in direct contact with the plate.
- The printed image is a reverse mirror image of the image on the plate
- Oil based inks are used.
- It costs a lot.

Silkscreen

Silk screen printing utilises a fine mesh stretched screen, with the image stencilled onto the screen surface, using hand cut stencils or photo exposure screen making methods. Ink is puddled onto the screen and squashed through onto the paper beneath using a rubber squeegee.

Silkscreen printing, also called serigraphy, has been the favourite method for limited editions with below 500 prints in the edition. Usually editions number about 300. The process involves making screens and printing one colour at a time, with a different screen for each required colour. An original silk screen might use 50 or more screens to build up the image. Each colour might take a day to print onto your 300 pieces of expensive heavy weight paper. That meant that a 50-colour print would take 50 days to print. You were obliged by the technology to print all 300 at the same time.

A variety of inks can be used including dense opaque inks, which will cover lower layers in the process, or fluorescent or metallic inks for startling effects.

As you can see there are characteristics of a silk-screen,

- The process prints one colour at a time.
- The paper is in direct contact with the screen.
- The printed image is a positive of the screen.
- A build up of thick ink will add a texture to the paper surface.

Commercially silk-screen printing has been used for very large paper sizes where printing presses are not suitable. Such uses would include outdoor hoarding posters and signs.

Another use for silkscreen techniques is where the surface to be printed would not work on a litho press like advertising banners, textiles, fabrics, or even sides of vehicles.

GICLEE

Giclee or inkjet printing

"Giclee" (pronounced Jee Clay), from the French for little squirt.

A "giclee" print is a piece of printed artwork, or photograph, produced by using a high quality digital inkjet printer.

A bit of giclee history

The pop star Graham Nash, of Crosby Stills Nash and Young fame, was a keen photographer and wanted to find a way to make large prints of his photographs. He explored the possibility of using an Iris proofing machine for the purpose, and with some adaptations the inkjet print onto high quality watercolour paper was developed.

The early pioneers used print machines that had been developed initially for the very big machine printers to get proofing done. A printer accepting a job to say print a magazine run would need to print a few proof copies before the production run. These would be sent for approval to the client. The cost of starting up a huge Heidelberg four colour printer was daunting so proofing print machines were vital.

The machines were only capable of printing a maximum of a meter square of paper at a time using a big drum, with paper attached. The drum spun round at high speed and the print heads moved slowly across the print.

The machines were very slow often taking an hour to print one A0 print sheet. The machines could cost £50,000.00 each and the paper might have been £10 a sheet.

The inks used were four colour dye-based inks, so the prints were likely to fade very quickly if exposed to sunlight. This did not matter for the proofing purpose of the machine but it was very bad for exhibition photos.

In the late nineties flat bed inkjet printers, capable of printing from a roll of paper, and using pigmented inks, were tested and found to give a promised life of 20 – 30 years before noticeable fading. Print machine makers include Epson, Mutoh, Mimaki and Roland.

The inks used have to be specially formulated and compatible with the extreme fineness of the printer head that spurts jets of ink in minute droplets at a resolution of 1440dpi or more. Epson and Lyson supply many of the ink-sets that have been tested. The paper or canvas that is used is specially prepared to accept this type of printing mechanism and ink-set. Again Epson and Lyson produce tested papers, and Hahnemuhle supply a range including a special canvas.

When Epson bought out their 7600 and 9600 models, with Ultrachrome pigmented ink-set lasting 80 + years, at very affordable prices, then the world of fine art publishing was changed for ever.

In 2003 Epson announced a new A2 printer [4000] that uses the Epson Ultrachrome ink-set.

Lightfastness in a giclee print

Early inkjet prints in the mid 1990's were disappointingly fugitive with noticeable fading occurring very quickly. Improvements have been made in the inks used and the paper or canvas substrate. It was found that it is crucial that the combination of machine, ink-set and substrate is compatible and tested as a whole. Recent tests show that the resulting print can be lightfast to very high levels with a minimum of six on the Blue Wool test.

The latest results show life expectancy rates of 100 to 200 years for some giclee prints. When printed on good quality heavyweight art paper the print should possess archival standards of permanence comparable or better than other collectable artwork.

Quality

The visual quality of the print result is extremely high with seeming continuous tone prints without dots, lines or barring. The colour saturation and definition can be stunning.

Benefits and disadvantages

One advantage that digital printing offers to the artist and publisher is that the edition can be printed on demand. Giclee images are recorded as a digital file and can be produced on a giclee printer singly, or more, whenever required. The prints will be exactly the same at the start and end of a print run, even if the run is interrupted and printed on different occasions. This means that the high cost and risk of producing a complete print edition all at once is avoided.

A second advantage to the artist and publisher is the control available by manipulation of the digital file. Using special software it is possible to tweak and alter the original image to improve the size, colour, tone and other qualities of the image.

It is also possible to design or create the print image completely on a computer using designer software such as Adobe PhotoShop, thus producing effects that could not be hand made in the studio using paint or ink.

However, the costs per giclee print remain quite high because the paper, ink machinery and specialist time involved are expensive.

But remember that before giclee became available the cost of producing one of your pictures in a printed form was very high indeed. The cost included photography, and scanning, followed by proofing, and finally printing, the whole edition in one go.

Conclusion

The effect of print-on-demand production affects the quantity and quality of published art images as more artists publish "giclee" editions.

Galleries have more choice and the collecting public are stimulated by wider choice and better quality art.

Publishers are freed from the necessity to hold large stocks.

Giclee prints are a radically new way that artists can produce art, publishers can supply art, and museums, galleries and collectors can display or own high quality art.

ISSUE NUMBER FOUR
Do it yourself, or get published by one of the big boys.

Getting published.

The South African artist Natasha Barnes has said that getting published by many publishing houses worldwide has not made her rich, but it has made her famous.

The problem with getting published by a publisher is that you are likely to get no more than 10% of the wholesale price. That is 5% of the retail. You really have to have an image selling very well to get much financial reward.

But the benefit of having your work seen in established print catalogues and at trade fairs is that your name and painting style is recognised by the art trade.

Do it your self

As previously mentioned the first advantage of publishing yourself is financial. You will get 50% of the retail price if you sell to a gallery direct. But you have got to do the selling and distribution yourself as well.

Traditional print making

Traditional old-fashioned print makers are craftsmen printing small editions, and usually issuing limited editions.

The commercial publishing world has been governed by the big publishing houses, which have the capital and distribution networks.

A revolution in publishing

Then along came usable giclee technology in the mid 90's.

The rise of giclee technology has unleashed a whole new force into the print market, namely self-publishing artists.

Using a bureau or buy a machine

So do you invest in a machine or do you go to a bureau to get the prints done for you?

Well the cheapest new giclee type of machine would set you back £450. It will print onto a maximum paper size of 13" x 19", [A3+].

A machine capable of printing A2 will set you back about £1500, and an A1 machine would be about £3000 with a service contract, and the A0 machine with a 44" wide carriage capable of printing very big prints will cost £6000 including a 3 year service contract.

If you go to a bureau it will probably cost you about £100 for scanning and the first print. You can then sell the print and ask for more prints from the same file. They will be identical to the first print even if you order them one at a time over the following year or so. A1 prints will cost you about £35 each, and smaller sizes would be proportionally less. You may have to make each order up to the equivalent of an A1, and obviously postage costs will bump up the unit price quite a bit if you buy them one at a time.

So it is probably a good idea to use a bureau to start with and only when you have made enough profit from bureau printed images will you invest in your own machine. Then you will find that the unit price drops but your wastage rate soars as you learn how to print yourself.

Eventually you could become a skilled home printer and become successful self-publishing artist.

Getting published by the big boys, revisited.

However, if you don't fancy the learning curve and technological white-knuckle ride, or you cannot face the task of selling and distribution, then maybe you should try to get published by someone else.

A big publisher will also be a big distributor, and could sell hundreds of your images all over the world.

But it isn't at all easy to get them interested. If you do your research and find the right publisher you will have to join the queue of hopefuls.

Fine Art Trade Guild Standards

The Fine Art Trade Guild, based in London, England, is the premier trade organisation for the fine art business in the world. The Guild sets standards for many facets of the fine art business as well as publishing the foremost trade magazine 'Art Business Today'.

Standards are set for:

- Lightfastness
- Paper weight
- Border/margin
- Certificate of authenticity

Worldwide members of the Guild include artists, art dealers, art galleries, picture framers, product suppliers, on-line galleries, artists' agents, and art groups.

Members get many benefits including low cost insurance, legal help, free magazine, financial help in exhibiting at overseas trade exhibitions, an online gallery for artists, a certification programme for framers, and a chance to participate in setting standards for the art industry. The full time professional staff are available for advice and help by telephone, email or fax.

Members are required to accept and abide by a code of practice that helps to ensure that the fine art business continues to be well respected.

Chapter Nine.....conclusion

There were four issues discussed in this chapter,

- Original or reproduction
- Limited edition or open edition
- Types of print making
- DIY or big boy publishers

GOLDEN RULE No 1:   **INVEST AND BELIEVE IN YOURSELF.**

GOLDEN RULE No 2:   **KEEP RECORDS.**

GOLDEN RULE No 3:   **AIM FOR QUALITY.**

GOLDEN RULE No 4:   **BE BUSINESSLIKE.**

GOLDEN RULE No 5:   **SEEK AND LISTEN TO EXPERT ADVICE.**

GOLDEN RULE No 6:   **FOCUS YOUR EFFORT.**

GOLDEN RULE No 7:   **JOIN UP, MEET PEOPLE, NETWORK.**

GOLDEN RULE No 8:   **BE PREPARED.**

GOLDEN RULE No 9:   **DON'T EXPECT A FAIRY GODMOTHER.**

GOLDEN RULE No 10:   **BE POSITIVE AND KEEP YOUR CHIN UP.**

GOLDEN RULE No 11:   **?**

GOLDEN RULE No 12:   **?**

CHAPTER TEN: Artistic license to make money?

Finding licensing deals.

What is licensing?

Licensing refers to the use of artwork for a secondary purpose. A good example would be the use of a painting as the image on a greetings card. Other typical fine art licensing can be found in calendars, posters, billboards, jigsaw puzzles, tea shirts, ceramics, mouse mats, book and magazine illustration, children's toys, holiday souvenirs, and other gift items.

The artist is the **licensor** and his/her work is licensed for use by the **licensee**.

Contracts

A contract between the licensor and licensee would typically be,

- for a set period of time,

- for an agreed specific usage

- for a specific geographic location

- for a fixed percentage or fee.

The contract should state when the artist gets paid. It might be that a up front payment is made with or without a percentage of later wholesale receipts, or it might be on a percentage of wholesale receipts only.

Most well established licensees will have a formal licensing agreement already in place, which the newbie artist will be expected to accept. It would be a good idea to talk to other artists, or get specialist legal help, before committing oneself to signing anything. Common pitfalls are that the licensee is a bad payer, or will fail to tell the artist of all sales of the licensed image, or will commit to deals that are not in the artist's best interest.

Agencies

Established licensing agencies exist which set out to find good deals for the artwork and share the spoils with the artist in exchange for doing the research, selling, checking and invoicing of the manufacturer.

Some of these agencies are off shoots of well-established fine art publishing companies themselves. Artists who are published by a print publisher can add to their income by agreeing that the publisher may look for other deals on the artist's behalf. They might have contacts and credibility for art licensing that you as a freelance would never equal. But you will probably have to give them at least half of the licensing income.

Other agencies are specialist-licensing businesses that will also be licensing personalities, authors, historic places, special events and the like. They will be very well versed in the uses and income available from the licensing trade.

The licensing business is huge.

Many millions of dollars/pounds/euros/yen per year are spent in this thriving sector of the international market in goods of many varieties, and a specialist licensing agency will be after a share.

Income streams

However, [sigh] the way to get a share of this multi million-dollar bean-feast is quite tricky. You as an artist will be well advised to paint pictures and sell them first, and maybe try dabbling in the hand-made greetings card business when possible. That is unless you hit upon a good set of images, happen across a good agent, who finds a good licensor for your work. Then you could do well, very well in fact.

At the time of writing this the working fee for a greetings card image is £250 to £350 for selling the rights to use an image for a couple of years solely as a greetings card.

The artist can usually also negotiate to get a small supply [say 100] of cards as a bonus, which he/she can sell at exhibitions for another £100 or so.

Fortunately the greetings card industry often produces cards in sets of four or six, or even a dozen. So your income from a good set of images might be £1500 or more. Also greetings card publishers, and that includes the massive Christmas card market, will want a supply of new images to appeal to their buyers every year.

The calendar market is another place where you might get six or twelve, or even thirteen if you include a cover image, at once. The calendar market works very far in advance and you might be able to get an income for calendar images all year round even though the product really only sells in December.

The artists Terry Harrison says that he makes a huge supplement to his income from the royalties derived from his images used on jigsaw puzzles.

Copyright issues

As you may already realise, in the UK you own the copyright of your own art. This is automatic and you don't have to do anything to register it. If you sell the art piece to anyone else you retain the copyright even when some one else owns the actual art-piece. When a buyer buys your pictures they do not buy the copyright as well, unless you also sell them the right to copy the art [copyright]. The copyright can only be transferred, from you to any one else, with your agreement in writing.

A verbal agreement for transfer of copyright is not binding in law in the UK.

If you die, then the copyright remains the property of your estate for another 75 years.

This copyright law will be different in other countries.

The Fine Art Trade Guild standards for a 'limited edition' print stipulate that the image will not be used for any other purpose other than publicity or in a book.

If you have published a print as a 'limited edition' then that image must not be used as a poster or a card or a calendar. If you have already used an image as a greetings card or in a calendar you should not use the image as a print that claims to be a 'limited edition'.

Chapter Ten...conclusion

A super professional artist can expect to make some good money from licensing.

<u>GOLDEN RULE No 1:</u>   <u>INVEST AND BELIEVE IN YOURSELF.</u>

<u>GOLDEN RULE No 2:</u>   <u>KEEP RECORDS.</u>

<u>GOLDEN RULE No 3:</u>   <u>AIM FOR QUALITY.</u>

<u>GOLDEN RULE No 4:</u>   <u>BE BUSINESSLIKE.</u>

<u>GOLDEN RULE No 5:</u>   <u>SEEK AND LISTEN TO EXPERT ADVICE.</u>

<u>GOLDEN RULE No 6:</u>   <u>FOCUS YOUR EFFORT.</u>

<u>GOLDEN RULE No 7:</u>   <u>JOIN UP, MEET PEOPLE, NETWORK.</u>

<u>GOLDEN RULE No 8:</u>   <u>BE PREPARED.</u>

<u>GOLDEN RULE No 9:</u>   <u>DON'T EXPECT A FAIRY GODMOTHER.</u>

<u>GOLDEN RULE No 10:</u>   <u>BE POSITIVE AND KEEP YOUR CHIN UP.</u>

<u>GOLDEN RULE No 11:</u>   ?

<u>GOLDEN RULE No 12:</u>   ?

CHAPTER ELEVEN: A matter of principle

Maximising your income and profit.

Leverage

When you paint a picture once and sell it once then you have a basic simple business model. Make and sell once.

But you can paint a picture, photograph it, scan it, and publish it, then sell the original, **AND**, then also sell the prints over time. You have applied leverage to the original 'make and sell once' business model.

Many forms of leverage are available. They imply that you will get a bigger and better income than the basic income. Publishing and licensing are the two most likely forms of leverage for you as an artist.

Your income from a simple paint once and sell once operation may be multiplied many fold by publishing prints of your work.

Lateral and Vertical expansion

When you paint a picture once and sell it once then you have a basic simple business model. Make and sell once. You expand by painting more and selling more, one at a time.

But, as an example, you may also frame the picture, and in setting up the framing side of your manufacture you may be able to frame other things for your client.

Or you may be able to sell the work of other artists to the same client and make a percentage from the sale. That is lateral expansion. Lateral expansion looks at the other ways that your business can develop on the same level as you with a wider range of goods.

Vertical expansion looks at developing the your business by also doing yourself the things that come before or after your production.

An example of expanding vertically could be by buying the business that supplies you with canvases, or the established gallery that sells your work, or setting up a business that publishes your work.

Or you might do both of these and expand laterally and vertically by opening a small framing shop and art gallery that sells your own work and other artists work and does picture and mirror framing as well. You could also print and publish your own and other artists works from the gallery.

That is an example of lateral and vertical expansion. Many artists do this.

Genghis Khan principle

The so-called Genghis Khan principle in business focuses on the commonest reason why businesses fail, that is lack of profits. Talk about the blinding bleeding obvious. But lack of profits comes from lack of sales surely! Not so according to the authors of this strategy.

Many businesses strive after turnover increase as a way of getting more profit, and cut selling price to increase turnover. Whereas, the GK principle concentrates on **maximising the profit margin**, which is the difference between manufacture plus overhead costs, and sales prices.

Basically the GK principle says that if you have a business model with a high profit margin you can absorb fluctuations in sales volume, and you can afford to invest more on production or expansion in the good times.

The GK principle encourages the manufacturer to survive and prosper by selling at the highest price possible, and not at the lowest price possible.

Do not chase turnover to the detriment of profit margins.

80/20 split principle

We have already touched on the eighty-twenty split principle in a previous chapter. It is well worth repeating because you can apply this principle to many of your problems, not just sales.

The 80/20 idea is that you look at your business and your life with a scalpel that seeks a schism that divides your analysis between 80% and 20%. The eighty percent perspective will be focused on one factor that is opposite to the 20% perspective.

Then you find another perspectival pairing that applies to the first pairing... got this so far?

Then you cross reference the dual aspect factors so that you explain the phenomenon of a ratio between larger and smaller factors. So the larger sector and the smaller sectors can be cross-referenced and conclusions drawn between the factors and sectors involved. Ha! Easy really.

In other words **if** your income from sales at a private view comes from selling **four fifths** of your pictures to **one fifth** of your invited exhibition visitors, then you can work out that only **one fifth** of your income is derived from pictures that are selling to **four fifths** of your guests.

So analyse the difference between the one fifth who buy and the four fifths who buy a lot less. Then concentrate future efforts on those unique characteristics held by the one fifth and ignore the different characteristics of the four fifths.

You will notice the '**if**' in the first sentence of this paragraph. This 80/20 principle says that there is no question about it, there is such a split, and it is up to you to find it.

So when you come across a sales problem, or a distribution problem, or a production problem, then use the 80/20 split analysis to figure out what are your priorities.

An example and variation of this principle has been said by others in another way like this,

> Split your viewers into three camps
>
> those who like your work maybe one quarter
>
> those dislike your work maybe one quarter
>
> those who don't care
>
> So 25% of your viewers like your work.
>
> You should concentrate on them, and not on the 75% who would be much more difficult to sell to.

Can you see the similarity between the 80/20 approach and this?

Sizzle not sausage

It is an old adage in sales that you should "sell the sizzle not the sausage". It is not just 'a sausage' it is a 'sausage that sizzles and smells wonderful, it tastes succulent and juicy, and it looks good on the plate, and it does you good by building muscle, and a host of other benefits'. You will sell more because you are changing the way to look at the product. You are showing a positive bonus to the potential buyer.

In other words when you are describing your pictures, or your ability to design a greetings card, or the venue of your latest exhibition, you should be emphasising the good feelings and good things that are bonuses rather than just the simple product or fact itself.

You should look for the sizzles in your art business and enthusiastically share them with your prospective buyers. You should be enthusiastic about everything you sell or thing that you do. You should tell yourself that there are sizzles in all your work, even in the more mundane record keeping, or picture delivery, or cleaning the studio floor. Then sell them to yourself.

Move the wardrobe

An old friend of mine who went on to become a very successful artist used to work in a furniture shop when he left art-college. He tells the story of one of the old timers in the store who showed him the simplest of sales ploys in the book. If a customer professed a passing interest in a small coffee table the old timer would be very helpful and get help to move a large wardrobe away from the coffee table to let the customer have a better view. It was not necessary to move the wardrobe because it would have been easier to ask the customer to change position. But the act of struggling to please the customer forged a bond and a commitment between the customer and the salesman. The customer had to wait for the wardrobe to be moved and so spent more time thinking about the coffee table.

You don't have to literally move wardrobes to make a positive connection with your customer/collector of course. But maybe you can take a picture off the wall and move it to another viewing position while your prospective customer waits. Or maybe you can take the picture round to the customer's house in the evening to see what it looks like at home.

Struggle a bit, and be seen to struggle a bit, that is the principle here.

1001 nails principle

If you go to get a thousand nails from an ironmonger for £10, and when you get home you count the nails only to find that you have been sold 999, then you will be mightily upset wont you? However, if you find that you have 1001 nails then you will be as pleased as Punch. The difference is just two nails.

This principle says that for just two nails you will get many happy customers and repeat customers. Simple really!

But easy to forget.

The Liberace principle

The story goes that the flamboyant pianist Liberace was facing a setback early in his career as a show pianist. Bookings were not coming in and money was tight. His agent called him to the office and suggested that Liberace reduced his booking fee to try to get more interest. From $300 to $200.

Liberace refused. He insisted instead that his asking fee should be doubled to $600 per session, as he needed extra income to cover the slow booking income.

A little later his agent called to say that the bookings were still rather slow, and Liberace once again insisted that the rate was doubled again to $1200.

Bookings picked up, his diary was filled, and Liberace never looked back.

Because his prices increased, people accepted that Liberace was worth the huge increase. That is just because that was the price asked.

Recently I heard of a lecturer who wished to get out of the business of giving talks and concentrate on writing a book. He upped his fee from $1000 to $20,000 overnight. That is a twenty times increase. He expected to price himself out of the lecture business and get himself the time for the book. In fact the opposite happened. His bookings grew in demand and he was more popular than ever. Of course he continued with the lectures and the book will have to wait.

GOLDEN RULE No 11: BE COURAGEOUS, GRAB OPPORTUNITIES

You don't have to be foolhardy but you must be brave. The life of an artist is one of self-discipline and self-belief, interspersed by bouts of failure and doubt. You will get over the troughs and bad bits by being courageous. Keep your eye on your goals, and grab any opportunity whenever it comes along. They do come along.

Chapter Eleven ......conclusion

The principles and business ideas in this chapter will help you sort out those unique individual problems where you have to apply a bit of common sense.

GOLDEN RULE No 1:   INVEST AND BELIEVE IN YOURSELF.

GOLDEN RULE No 2:   KEEP RECORDS.

GOLDEN RULE No 3:   AIM FOR QUALITY.

GOLDEN RULE No 4:   BE BUSINESSLIKE.

GOLDEN RULE No 5:   SEEK AND LISTEN TO EXPERT ADVICE.

GOLDEN RULE No 6:   FOCUS YOUR EFFORT.

GOLDEN RULE No 7:   JOIN UP, MEET PEOPLE, NETWORK.

GOLDEN RULE No 8:   BE PREPARED.

GOLDEN RULE No 9:   DON'T EXPECT FAIRY GODMOTHERS.

GOLDEN RULE No 10:   BE POSITIVE AND KEEP YOUR CHIN UP.

GOLDEN RULE No 11:   BE COURAGEOUS, GRAB OPPORTUNITIES.

GOLDEN RULE No 12:   ?

CHAPTER TWELVE: And for my next trick

What comes next...
...and the final Golden Rule.

Website

You should get yourself a website. In the modern world any business without a website is hoping that it will be the one exception to the rule. Oh dear! A picture springs to mind of an ostrich and a bucket of sand.

If you want to find out something nowadays, your first response is most likely to go to your computer and look it up in Google. If not, it will be soon.

So if you want to be sure that you will be seen then you should get your own website. You could get a free site that had an address something like

www.theacmeartgallery/oneoftheartists//abc/subsection/obscurebutfree/smith.com

where your name appears at the end of a load of stuff.

Or if you get your own site you might get www.smith.com

Oh dear again, if your name really is 'smith' then you wont get it because it is already taken. So go for something else that hasn't been taken yet. But be quick. You should have done this ages ago.

And do try to get a dot com address if possible. Look professional. You can have the dot UK version as well of course with both domains pointing to the same site.

I have got   www.colinruffell.com

www.franslade.com

www.crabfish.com

www.crabfish.co.uk

And a couple more domains that serve different purposes.

All point to the same website where my wife Fran Slade and I share our portfolios and webspace.

That is what you should be doing with a website, displaying your portfolio of work.

You should have a biography and if possible get a shopping cart so that you can make some sales.

There are loads of cheap packages for hosting and domain name registering. If you haven't already got your website then treat this as a priority.

Cards

You should have some business cards with your contact details, such as name, address, telephone(s), fax number, and of course your website address and email address. And make sure that it says that you are an artist.

You should always carry them with you, and you should give them out to anyone that says some thing like "Oh you're an artist are you".

Postcards

In some ways a full colour postcard with one of your best images printed on one side and the other-side blank except for a line with your name and website address is a good idea. You can give this away with your business card, or you can sell it at shows for a very small price and still make a profit.

You can use postcards too as invites to shows by sticking a simple label on the back with the show details on. Even as an invite to a private view.

It could be the tiny extra thing that you include in your sales package when you send out prints that you have sold on your website.

The cost for 500 or a thousand cards is very small compared to the benefit that you can get from the investment.

Brochures

Brochures are more expensive than business cards or postcards, and can be a big expense at trade shows. You may want to try a mail shot where you send out brochures showing your work to prospective customers like galleries or interior designers.

A design that is versatile would be very cost effective. Such as a beautiful cover/folder with your name and contact details and a sample picture, plus loose sheets that you can print on your home printer to insert for different occasions.

You will find this very useful for exhibitions where you just insert a price list and biography, or trade shows where you insert a trade price list and terms, or a juried show application where you insert a few pictures and slides.

Books

There is a tradition for publishing houses to produce big coffee table tomes about famous artists. Some galleries produce smaller biographical stiff cover books to impress their clientele. These books would be an extravagant vanity for the professional artist to self-publish. But they do look good and help sales especially as gallery gifts to the best collectors.

However, maybe you are reading an e-book here. Possibly there is a new market for self-publishing e-books that show a catalogue of the artist's works, plus the usual biographical stuff, and a manifesto, or interview with the artist. These might not be very different to a good website, or a good website is not so very different to a potential e-book. A good quality e-book could be made available as a CD to do the same job as the expensive tome of previous years. We live in exciting times!

CD's

Many, if not most, computers will write a CD nowadays. A CD can be written that mirrors your website or an e-book very easily and cheaply. A CD can be sent by mail anywhere in the world at very low cost.

So why not offer CD's as an alternative to brochures or even books?

It is up to you whether you charge for them or send them at cost or even free. That depends on the content or the message on the CD.

One disadvantage of a CD is that it is not so easy to see what it is all about from the cover, so you will need to be able to print on the CD. If you have to get a new desktop printer in the near future look for one that will print onto CD's and you should get your money back a bit quicker.

Videos.

Even better than an e-book or CD showing the artists biography and catalogues could be a video showing the artist at work and being interviewed.

Such a video would be very good for use as an entry tool to juried shows, as a press aid to attract free editorial coverage, as a selling aid to attract the best affluent collectors, as well as something to give away at Christmas to your family.

TV

If you have made a good video why not try to sell the idea to a TV company? TV companies are looking for 25-minute slots all the time.

One successful artist that I know here in the UK, Terry Harrison, sells his own product on TV shopping channels. He actually developed a range of three special green colours, and a violet 'shadow' colour, that he used in his watercolour paintings. He got a paint company to make these colours and put them into tubes for him. He sells these at his demonstrations and at special artists exhibitions.

You can see his product on www.terryharrison.com

That is a good example of expansion laterally and vertically.

Press release

You should prepare yourself a simple press pack that you could update whenever there is an opportunity or special occasion.

At the top of the press pack should be a 'press release'.

Here is the simple formula. Start with the words PRESS RELEASE. Follow this with the release date from when it can be used.

The title should be next, followed by the most important point of the message. Keep the press release down to four or five paragraphs on one page, and remember to put your contact details at the bottom.

Add a photograph or two with full contact details and title on every one.

Do your research and aim your press pack at the most appropriate publication first.

Many magazines and local papers will willingly use a press release if properly prepared and if the story has interest and is well written. It saves the editor a lot of time!

Free editorial coverage

If you find that you can write about your art you might get asked to write about other arty things as well. Book reviews, exhibitions, artists products can all be your special subject. Each time you get into the press you add to your stock of credibility with the buyers who read the publication. So if you sell to the art trade you should attempt to supply the art trade press with free comment and editorial. If you paint dogs, and sell to dog lovers, why not supply the doggy trade magazines with material. Another tack would be to write to the letters column of the magazines that you target.

Advertising

When you reach the giddy heights of success you will be asked to advertise in various magazines and papers. Have a good look before you budget to spend money here. You could be doing yourself a bit of good but it also might be money wasted.

The best advertisements to consider early in your professional career will be for exhibitions or open houses/studios in a paper that is listing other similar adverts. If you pay for a picture while others just pay for a listing you could be doing some good.

Someone once told me, in a former life when I worked in advertising, that "advertising is like wetting yourself whilst wearing dark trousers. It feels wonderful at first but you don't know whether it shows or not".

Later in your career you will consider advertising in special trade show catalogues. But wait until you can afford to use the money without getting an immediate return.

I met an artist in Australia once who painted a series of landscapes of his beautiful countryside. He published a series of prints from the originals. He made a good few bucks by advertising his prints in local Ozzy newspapers. Whenever he needed some money he would just put an ad into a paper that hadn't seen his stuff before. So it can work if you specialise.

Internet chatrooms and forums

Chatrooms and forums are said to be the cheapest and quickest way to get your self or your product noticed. How did you hear about this book? Was it through a chatroom? If it wasn't, then you heard about it after someone else heard it in a chat room, because the first way that this book will be publicised will be by messages sent to chat rooms with a sig file from www.howtobeanartist.com

Maybe if you are reading this then the point has been proved.

Internet auctions

There is a good e-book about how to sell your art on ebay. I haven't tried the tips in it yet! But I bought it and it looks like a goldmine if you go that course.

I was inspired, so I then got down to it, and wrote my own e-book instead.

The book is by Brett Raven. Click here to get his book.

http://hop.clickbank.net/?crabfish/ebayartist

Speaker engagements

A few artists that I know make extra money by speaking at seminars or trade shows. Others do it for free to get the publicity.

Awards

Awards for artists are available from various sources. The Paul Hamlyn Foundation came up first when I searched on Google. They give away £30,000 per year to five artists.

The Arts & Business initiative have details about awards on their website

http://www.aandb.co.uk/

Or try

 http://www.publicartonline.org.uk/project/index.php

My own art group in Brighton successfully asked for funding to write and publish a book about the history of the Artists Open House movement from the lottery fund. Another artist was successful in obtaining funding from the same fund for an exhibition project to link medical science and art, which I was glad to participate in.

Bursaries,Residencies

Grants

A search on Google should be your first resource to find any free money available to you in your position. Getting free money has been done many times. I know of one artist who applies to several every year and he has been successful at least three times. He travelled to the Caribbean for a spell of painting in the sun, and then became an artist in residence at a big London gallery, and had all his debts paid off by an artist's charity, on different occasions. So it can be done, you just have to ask and follow the procedure.

Visit trade shows

Any artist with ambitions to supply the art trade business should make a regular pilgrimage to the Spring Fair at the NEC in Birmingham. It is held in February and is open to the trade only. You are in the fine art trade now so contact the organizers for a pass and details about the opening days.

http://www.springfair.com

Another good show to visit is in New York at ArtExpo in March.

The Fine Art Trade Guild in London has a list of all trade shows of interest to budding artists.

http://www.fineart.co.uk

Visit specialist shows e.g. horse, dogs, gardening, boats, cars.

If your art is about a special subject, and you are aiming at a special niche in the market you should visit the appropriate trade show. For instance if you paint horses then go to horse shows. You will often find that other specialist artists have booked themselves space at these shows to sell to this market.

Visit libraries and Subscribe to magazines

Visit your local reading room at the library and find the specialist magazines for your market niche if possible. Subscribe to any that seem to be catering for the same group that you wish to attract. This way you find out what the latest interests and buzzwords are, and you can make sure that you can talk knowledgably to your potential clients. Consider submitting editorial press releases to the same magazines to get free coverage, or even take small advertisements in them if you find that other artists are doing the same. It might be a good idea to phone any other artist who you find like this and asking if it is worthwhile. Some artists can be very helpful to newcomers.

Join web forums

The mushrooming connectivity and increase in speed from broadband on the internet, has meant that many world wide web forums exist for you in whatever niche you choose. Search yahoo groups for the groups that suit you. Join up and start a dialogue if possible. You will certainly learn a great deal, and you could get in touch with many new potential buyers.

The final rule

As an artist you are something quite special. You are valued in society because you are a visionary providing joy and insight into the creative world.

Many non-artists would cut off their right arm to be like you. They will open up their homes and wallets to get a little second hand feel of what it is like being an artist.

You have to consider the position of all the other artists in the world, now, in the past, and in the future. You can make it better for art and artists or you can make it worse. You make it better by being efficient, successful, and not wasting your talent. You can make it worse by squandering the opportunity by hesitating or being timid. Be brave.

You have a responsibility to yourself to do the job properly. You will really enjoy the excitement and uncertainty and tension and buzz that a full time artist's life can bring.

So what is the ultimate golden rule?

You are in charge and you are unique. So you should decide for yourself whether or not to follow any rules, for how long, or even if at all. The previous eleven golden rules could be tried out until you are on your way to the success, which can be yours if you want it. They should get you up to speed down the runway of your full time career as an artist. But whenever you feel that you are ready, then pull back the joystick and take off from the rulebook. Abandon the previous eleven golden rules and realise that there are no golden rules for artists.

GOLDEN RULE No 12: THERE ARE NO GOLDEN RULES

Go for it!

Chapter Twelve......conclusion

Chapter Twelve has shown you many activities any one of which could make all the difference between failure and success. The final Golden Rule is about your freedom to make choices.

GOLDEN RULE No 1:   **INVEST AND BELIEVE IN YOURSELF.**

GOLDEN RULE No 2:   **KEEP RECORDS.**

GOLDEN RULE No 3:   **AIM FOR QUALITY.**

GOLDEN RULE No 4:   **BE BUSINESSLIKE.**

GOLDEN RULE No 5:   **SEEK AND LISTEN TO EXPERT ADVICE.**

GOLDEN RULE No 6:   **FOCUS YOUR EFFORT.**

GOLDEN RULE No 7:   **JOIN UP, MEET PEOPLE, NETWORK.**

GOLDEN RULE No 8:   **BE PREPARED.**

GOLDEN RULE No 9:   **DON'T EXPECT FAIRY GODMOTHERS.**

GOLDEN RULE No 10:   **BE POSITIVE AND KEEP YOUR CHIN UP.**

GOLDEN RULE No 11:   **BE COURAGEOUS, GRAB OPPORTUNITIES.**

GOLDEN RULE No 12:   **THERE ARE NO GOLDEN RULES.**

Who is this author?

Something about Colin Ruffell to show that he might just know what he is talking about.

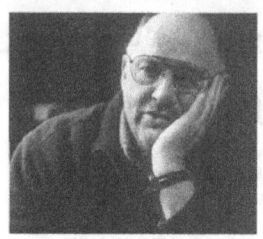

•

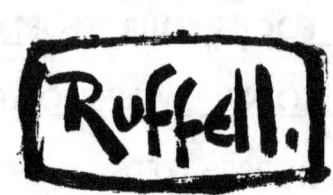

www.crabfish.com

Colin Ruffell, the blurb

Colin Ruffell was born in 1939, then he was bombed, evacuated, educated, expelled, repatriated, married, bred, qualified and taught; an interesting if chaotic childhood and adolescence. In 1965, he became a professional artist, and is proud and happy to have survived ever since.

He has qualifications from two Art Colleges in painting, design and printmaking, and the Open University in psychology and aesthetics, plus a reasonably clean driving license.

He has founded, led or organised the following; Spectrum Studios, Artists in Action, Bayswater Road Artists Association, 9-Plus Artists Group, Buckingham Fine Art Ltd., Brighton Artists Workshop, European Fine Art Ltd., The Fiveways Artists Group, and Crabfish Ltd.

Exhibited in; England, Scotland, Wales, Sweden, Germany, Holland, U.S.A., Canada, Japan, Venezuela, and Australia, plus works in private and corporate collections worldwide. Published by: The Art Group, ArtSmile, Buckingham Fine Art, Canadian Art Prints, Ecosse Fine Art, Edinburgh Arts, Hibell Japan, London Contemporary Art, Winn Devon UK.

He likes cooking, drinking, eating, playing with his grandchildren, which is harmless. However, beware, because he also likes talking about the archeo-psychic ego state, or biological determinism, and he goes bird watching.

He has been a pioneer of changing techniques for artists. He was one of the first guinea pig students in England to use the revolutionary medium of artists acrylic paint, and he has been a consistent advocate ever since. In the nineties he spotted the potential of giclee printmaking, and the Internet as exhibition space. His enthusiasm led The Fine Art Trade Guild to elect him firstly as a Court Member and then as Chair of The Guilds Printers and Publishers Committee where he is involved in setting worldwide standards for the fine art publishing industry.

His pictures are varied. He paints in many styles. Some images are childlike and amusing, others are traditional landscapes, and yet more are complex modernist abstract relationships of colour, texture and shape. He claims that he paints in explosive bursts, necessarily punctuated by long spells of getting ready or recovery from the last effort.

Colin Ruffell, the bare facts;

Born 13th July 1939 in Kent England.

Married artist Fran Slade 1960

Hornsey Art College 1956-59.

Portsmouth Art College 1962-64 National Diploma in Design.

Open University 1984-96 BSc Hons

Art teacher Bedford 1964-65.

Founder Spectrum Studios Bedford 1965

Chairman Bayswater Road Artists Association 1972, 73

Founder Member 9+ Artists Group 1973

Exclusive contract with Seen Galleries London 1976, 77.

Exclusive contract with Sion Essex Fine Art 1978

Founder Brighton Artists Workshop 1978-

Member Fiveways Artists Group Brighton 1991-

Elected Director of The Fine Art Trade Guild UK [FATG] 2000

Chair FATG Fine Art Printers and Publishers Committee 2001 –

Managing Director Crabfish Ltd. 2002 –

Published by

Limited Editions Gallery

Buckingham Fine Art Ltd

London Contemporary Art

Royle Publications

The Paper House Group

Brighton Artists Workshop

Second Nature Ltd

Ecosse Fine Art

Edinburgh Arts

The Art Group

Winn Devon

Canadian Art prints

Hibell Japan

Artsmile

Collections and commissions

Ford Motor Company

Midland Bank

Rolls Royce

Jones Lang and Wootton

London and Paris Property Company

Cigna Services UK Ltd

House of Fraser

Elf Petroleum France

Virgin Atlantic

Cisco Systems

Exhibitions

1958	Embankment, Temple Gardens, London
1959	Young Contemporaries, London
1959	Arts Council, tour of Great Britain
1963	TUC HQ Congress House London
1963	Architects Association London
1966	Banbury Arts Festival

1966	Britain's Best", Rackhams, Birmingham
1966-8	G Plan Artists in Action, major UK cities.
1969	Bayswater Road, London
1973	9+ Group, Chenil Galleries, Chelsea, London
1973	"First One Man Show", Preston St Art Gallery, Brighton
1974	9+ Group, Caracas, Venezuela
1974	9+ Group, Osaka, Japan
1976	"Don't Stamp on Flowers", Seen Gallery, London
1977	One Man Show, Oak Tree Studio, Shipley
1977	One Man Show, Studio 18, St Helier, Jersey
1978	Mixed Show, Osborne Galleries, Brighton
1978	One man Show, The Coach House Gallery, Guernsey
1979	"Tre Naivester", Galleri Fenix, Gothenburg, Sweden
1980-98	Brighton Artists Workshop, Brighton
1983	"Naïve Art", Howard Street Gallery, Perth, Western Australia
1984	Mixed Show, Howard Street Gallery, Perth, Western Australia
1991-04	Fiveways Artists Group Open Houses, Brighton Festival
1992	Sussex Open, Brighton
1993	"Not the Royal Academy", Llewellyn Alexander Gallery, London
1994	Fiveways Artists Group Open Houses, Brighton Festival
1994	The London Exhibition, Art for Offices Gallery, London
1995	ArtExpo, New York. USA
1995	Dix et Sept, Greenwich Village, New York, USA
1996	Star Gallery, Lewes
1996-98	Blackheath Gallery, London John Arthur Gallery, Dorking Various galleries in UK
2000-03	Fine Art Trade Guild members on tour
2003	Hibell Galleries Japan
2003-04	Décor Expo New York

A Glossary of Arty Terms

Or "what do artists mean by...?"

This glossary contains mixed American and UK terms.

A

ABSTRACT; non-subjective art, art that utilises shape, colour and texture, without representing real objects.

ABSTRACT EXPRESSIONISM; An American style of painting that developed in the late 1940s. It had two branches, one called "Action painting" and the other "Color Field painting". Both were characterized by a non-representational style that stressed psychological or emotional meaning.

ACADEMIC; A term applied to any kind of art that stresses the use of accepted rules for technique and form organization. It represents the exact opposite of the creative approach, which results in a vital, individualistic style of expression.

ACRYLIC PAINT; pigment suspended in acrylic resin, water soluble before dry, permanent after drying.

ACTION PAINTING; An Abstract-Expressionist style that involves dripping, spraying and brushing techniques in the application of pigment to the painting surface.

AESTHETIC; Having to do with the pleasurable and beautiful as opposed to the useful or scientific. An aesthetic response is the perception and enjoyment of a work of art.

AESTHETICS; A compound of the philosophy, psychology, and sociology of art and to do with the nature of beauty and its relation to human beings.

ARTISTS PROOF; [AP] term used to distinguish small number of perfect example prints from an edition. Usually extra 10% not included in the total number in a limited edition. Usually property of the artist and numbered in Roman numerals. [see **EDITION [LIMITED]**]

ARTWORK; original work by the artist for use in production of PRINTS etc..

ATMOSPHERIC (AERIAL) PERSPECTIVE; The illusion of deep space produced in graphic works by lightening values, softening details and textures, reducing value contrasts, and neutralizing colors in objects as they recede.

B

BINDER; The liquid medium that is mixed with pigment to form paint, or pastel sticks. The binder used for water-colour is gum arabic; oil paints are bound with oil, acrylics with a synthetic resin, and pastels with gum tragacanth.

C

CANVAS; traditional ground for oil or acrylic paintings. Usually GESSO'ed and stretched on STRETCHERS.

CHIAROSCURO; [15th century] light and dark in a painting, often well defined showing single light direction.

CHROMA; 1. The purity of color or its freedom from white, black, or gray. 2. The intensity of hue.

CHROMATIC; Pertaining to the presence of color.

CLASSICAL; Art forms that are characterized by a rational, controlled, clear, and intellectual approach.

COLLAGE; From the French word coller meaning, "to paste". A pictorialtechnique in which the artist creates the image, or a portion of it, by adhering real materials that possess actual textures to the picture-plane surface, often combining them with painted or drawn passages.

COLOUR; The visual response to the wavelengths of light identified as red, green, blue, etc.

COLOUR FIELD PAINTING; Another branch of Abstract Expressionism in which artists filled extremely canvases with bright color meant to involve the viewer psychologically. They created unified shapes, fields and/or symbols of the artists' personal feelings. The fields of color were flat in technique and bonded or integral to the surface.

COMPLEMENTARY COLORS; Two colors directly opposite each other on the color wheel. A primary color is complementary to a secondary color that is a mixture of the two remaining primaries.

COMPOSITION; An arrangement and/or structure of all the elements which achieve a unified whole. Often used interchangeably with the term design.

COMPUTER ENHANCED IMAGE; picture produced with one of its stages being in digital language using computer software. Awesome technology available to the advertising industry and graphic designers and increasingly available to FINE ARTISTS.

CONCEPTUAL PERCEPTION; Creative vision that derives from the imagination.

CONTENT; The expression, essential meaning, significance, or aesthetic value of a work of art. Content refers to the sensory, subjective, psychological, or emotional properties we feel in a work of art, as opposed to our perception of its descriptive aspects alone.

C.T.L.X. [COTOLAX] CONTIUOUS TONE LASER XEROGRAPH; high quality picture end product of computer technology involving dry pigment [toner] fixed by "melting" onto paper with LASER.

CUBISM; The name given to the painting style invented by Pablo Picasso and Georges Braque between 1906 and 1914. Cubists used multiple views of objects to create the effect of their three-dimensionality, while acknowledging the two-dimensional surface of the picture plane.

CULTURE; A set of learned ways of thinking and acting that characterizes a decision-making human group.

D

DADA; A nihilistic, anti-art, anti-everything art movement resulting from the social, political, and psychological dislocations of World War I. The movement, which literally means hobbyhorse, is important historically as a generating force for Surrealism. The Dada movement began in Zurich, Switzerland, in 1916.

DEALER SYSTEM; the system of FINE ART sale and distribution usually from galleries. Prestigious international dealers contract artists and provide salaries in exchange for promotion and exhibitions. Main effect is to provide art to wealthy collectors and public galleries, however side effect is to keep artists and general public apart, and put up prices.

DESIGN; A framework or scheme of construction on which artists base the nature of their total work. In a broader sense, design may be considered synonymous with the term form.

DE STIJL; A Dutch form of art featuring primary colors within a balanced structure of lines and rectangles. It was a style to perfectly express the higher mystical unity between humankind and the universe. Translated as the Style it was the form of abstraction developed by Piet Mondrian and Theo van Doesburg about 1914-17.

DILUENT; Liquids used to thin down paint, such as turpentine or white spirit of oils and water for water-based paints.

DISTRESSING; deliberate ageing effects applied to frames and furniture.

DRAWING; The art or act of representing something on a surface by means of lines and shades, as with a pencil, crayon, pen, chalk, compasses, etc. Also, a sketch, plan, picture or design made with such materials.

DRY BRUSH; A technique of applying the minimum of paint to the surface, usually with the bristles of the brush slightly splayed out.

E

EDITION [LIMITED]; published art works that are all exactly the same, usually published at the same time, and limited to quoted number. Pencil marking in fraction format, upper number is particular to that print and lower number is size of edition. The publisher undertakes not to produce more than edition size. The smaller the edition size the more rare and hence potential value. Edition sizes range from an edition of 2 to thousands. In practice editions over 750 have little if any extra value.

EDITION [OPEN]; an unlimited edition, usually un-numbered. Usually less expensive than limited editions. However this may be because the published method is such that pictures are produced to order one at a time rather than all at once. Open editions may therefore be more rare than limited editions.

ENGRAVING; pictures produced by cutting into surface of metal or wood plate to hold ink for printmaking.

ETCHING; similar to engraving but use is made of acid to etch into plate surface after image is inscribed onto surface which has been covered in acid resisting ground.

EXPRESSIONISM; A form of art in which there is a desire to express what is felt rather than perceived or reasoned. Expressionistic form is defined by an obvious exaggeration of natural objects for the purpose of emphasizing an emotion, mood, or concept. It can better be understood as a more vehement kind of Romanticism. The term is best applied to a movement in art of the early twentieth century, encompassing the Fauves and German groups, although it can be used to describe all art of this character.

F

FANTASTIC ART; Not a particular style or movement, but a term to describe the departure from accepted appearances or relationships for the sake of psychological expression in the arts. Fantasy may exist in any art style, but is usually thought of in connection with unencumbered flights of pictorial imagery, freely interpreted or invented.

FAT-OVER-LEAN; The traditional way of building up an oil painting; beginning with thin, non-oily paint (lean) and increasing the thickness and oil content as the painting proceeds. For any painting built up in a series of layers, this is very important. Thick, oily paint takes a long time to dry, a shrinks slightly in the process. If lean paint is laid over this, the top layer will dry first, and may crack as the lower layer shrinks.

FAUVES (FAUVISM); A name (meaning wild beasts) for an art movement that began in Paris, France, about 1905. It was expressionistic art in a general sense, but more decorative, orderly, and charming than German Expressionism.

FIGURATIVE PAINTING; A painting of something actual, as opposed to an abstract painting. The word does not imply the presence of human figures.

FORM; 1. The arbitrary organization or inventive arrangement of all the visual elements according to the principles that will develop unity in the artwork. 2. The total appearance or organization of the artwork.

FINE ART; the visual arts, which include painting, drawing, printmaking, sculpture and some performance art. Excludes other art forms such as poetry, literature, dance and music.

FRAME SIZE; in effect rebate size, measurements are traditionally the size of the canvas or panel in unglazed work, and the size of the glass in paper work under glass, not overall size.

G

GALLERY SYSTEM; see **DEALER SYSTEM** for international galleries. High Street galleries do not usually contract artists, selling instead mainly prints and some originals, but often relying on picture framing business to support the high rents and rates of central premises. Useful source of local art.

GESSO; mixture of chalk whiting and glue, which makes ideal surface for painting in oils or acrylics.

GICLEE; literally means little squirt in French. The latest digital printing technique enabling "print on demand". Originally term used by Iris printers but rapidly becoming generic term for top quality digital prints using archival quality inks on heavy weight paper or canvas.

GLAZING; 1. A technique of applying oil or acrylic color in thin, transparent layers so that the color beneath shows through, modifying the color of the glaze. 2. Fitting a sheet of glass in front of the picture to protect the picture surface.

GOLDEN MEAN; Perfect harmonious proportions that avoid extremes; the moderation between extremes.

GOLDEN SECTION; A traditional proportional system for visual harmony expressed when a line or area is divided into two so that the smaller.part is to the larger as the larger is to the whole. The ratio developed is 1:1.6180....or, roughly, 8:13.

GOUACHE; opaque watercolour, sometimes called designers colour. [see **WATER-COLOUR**]

GRAPHIC ARTIST; artists, designers and illustrators, often freelance, but employed in the publishing, media and advertising industries.

GRAPHICS; A form of artistic expression, usually on paper, through emphasis on lines, marks, or printed letters rather than on color. It includes everything from drawing through print-making of all kinds including the art of typesetting and book design. It also refers to illustrations, diagrams or designs accompanying printed matter.

GREEN ISSUES; growing concern of artists and public. Art materials, especially pigments, were until very recently very toxic while being used. Modern materials are much safer for the artist. Public concern has been expressed over the use of hard woods in picture frame making. Most frame designs are now available in renewable soft woods. Ask!

GROUND; surface on which painting or drawing is made, e.g. canvas, paper, panel.

GUM ARABIC; the binding agent for watercolour pigments, which is soluble in water, and does not lose solubility when dry. Hence water-colours are susceptible to damp and should be exhibited behind protective layer of glass and sealed at the back.

H

HATCHING; Repeated strokes of an art tool producing clustered lines (usually parallel) that create values. In cross -hatching similar lines pass over the hatched lines, following a different direction and usually resulting in darker values.

HUE; Designates the common name of a color and indicates its position in the spectrum or on the color wheel. Hue is determined by the specific wavelength of the color in a ray of light.

I

ILLUSIONISM; The imitation of visual reality created on the flat surface of the picture plane by the use of perspective, light-and-dark shading, etc.

ILLUSTRATION(AL); An art practice, usually commercial in character, that stresses anecdotes or story situations and stresses subject more than form.

INSTALLATION; A term used to describe an assemblage or environment constructed in the gallery specifically for a particular exhibition.

INTENSITY; The saturation, strength, or purity of color.

INTERMEDIATE; A color produced by a mixture of a primary color and a secondary color.

IMPASTO; thick paint applied with brush, palette knife or fingers etc..

IMPRESSIONISM; A movement of the late nineteenth century primarily connected with such painters as Claude Monet and Camille Pissarro. A form of realistic painting on the way in which changing aspects of light affect human vision; it challenged older models of such representation.

IMPRIMATURA; A layer of color applied to a ground, often used as a middle tone in a painting.

INK; usually any thin and runny colour using manufacturers secret formulas. Printing ink is usually more sticky and more greasy than writing or drawing ink. Indian ink is black and is traditionally used as a non-soluble drawing ink also known as Chinese ink.

J

K

L

LANDSCAPE FORMAT; any picture that is wider than tall. Pictures are usually measured with side measurements first and top and bottom measurement last. [see **PORTRAIT FORMAT**]

LASER PRINT; recent mechanised publishing process using the wonders of modern technology including computers and lasers to melt toner [dry ink] onto the surface to be printed. [see **XEROGRAPH**]

LINEAR PERSPECTIVE (GEOMETRIC); A system used to develop three-dimensional images on a two-dimensional surface; it develops the optical phenomenon of diminishing size by treating edges as converging parallel lines. They extend to a vanishing point or points on the horizon (eye-level) and recede from the viewer. (See **PERSPECTIVE**)

LITHOGRAPH; literally stone image. In lithography the surface that receives the image to be printed is not engraved but remains flat. The printing ink is attracted to areas that are made greasy and resisted by areas that are made wet with water. Originally large flat stones were used but nowadays the plates are usually metal [zinc] or plastic.

LOCAL (OBJECTIVE) COLOR; The color as seen in the objective world (green grass, blue sky, red barn, etc.).

LOCAL VALUE; The relative light or dark of a surface, seen in the objective world, that is independent of any effect created by the degree of light falling on it.

LOW-KEY COLOR; Any color which has a value level of middle gray or darker.

M

MAHLSTICK; A piece of bamboo or rod dowel rod with a pad at one end, used for steadying the hand when painting fine details.

MATT; American term for MOUNT.

MEDIUM; 1. The material used for painting (or drawing), i.e. oil, water-colour, acrylic, pastel. 2. Another term for binder , a substance used in the manufacture of paint. 3. Substances added to paint while working to make it thicker, thinner, more glossy, and so on. These may be traditional mediums such as poppy oil and linseed oil, or synthetic ones, such as Liquin, Wingel, or acrylic medium.

MIXED MEDIA; A painting or other work of art in which more than one medium and/or material is used; e.g. using acrylic, and water-colour in a single work.

MOBILE; A three-dimensional moving sculpture.

MODERN ART; The term modern art is applied to almost all progressive or avant-garde phases of art from the time of the Impressionists in the late 1880's to the growth of Postmodernism in the 1960's.

MODERNISM; An art form usually associated with the non-representational, formally organized branch of modern art, as opposed to the organic and/or fantastic branches.

MONOPRINT; one off print, often made by inking up a glass surface and pressing paper onto it. Each image is slightly different if process is repeated.

MOTIF; A designed unit or pattern that is repeated often enough in a total composition to make it a significant or dominant feature. Motif is similar to theme or melody in a musical composition.

MOUNT; card surround around paper picture to keep ink or paint surface from touching the glass. Usually decorated and integral part of the finished picture. Can be used by artist to sign picture.

MULTIPLE; any repeated reproduction of an original, including sculpture. [see **CHROMAGRAPH**, **PRINT** etc.]

N

NEGATIVE AREA(S); The unoccupied or empty space left after the artist has created the positive elements. However, when these areas have boundaries, they also function as design shapes in the total structure.

NEO-ABSTRACTION; Within the broad church of Post-modern art there exists a hard core of artists who have chosen to remain within the abstract manner. Most of them are influenced by the rich color work of such artists as Frank Stella and Al Held.

NEO-CLASSICISM; A style initiated in the late 1700's in France, which centred upon a reintroduction of Classical Greek and Roman forms of art, as then understood. It became the basis for the approved or official art of the French government until about the middle of the nineteenth century. The main exponents were Jacques-Louis David and Jean-Auguste Dominique Ingres.

NEO-EXPRESSIONISM; Dating from the early 1980's, this style reaffirmed the psychic emotionalism of the early twentieth-century Expressionism. It became perhaps the most distinctive direction in Postmodernism.

NON-REPRESENTATIONAL; A term used to define a range of work encompassing non-recognizable imagery that varies from pure abstraction (non-recognizable but derived from a recognizable object) to non-objective (not a product of the abstraction process, but deriving from the artist's mind).

O

OBJECTIVE (ART); That which is based, as near as possible, on physical actuality or optical perception. Such art tends to appear natural or real

OIL PAINT; traditionally the main binding agent for pigment in non glazed paintings was linseed or stand oil. When dry the colour is non-soluble and can be exposed to the atmosphere. Unfortunately the oil takes a long time to dry to full dryness and many modern artists prefer to use ACRYLIC paints which are soluble in water until dry which is only hours after application.

OPAQUE; Having cover power; not permitting the prepared surface or other colors to show through or other colors

ORIGINAL PAINTING; any artwork where the artist designs and applies the work.

ORIGINAL PRINT; tricky definition usually taken to mean any non-mechanical print made by the original artist and usually a numbered and limited edition. Often on very good quality paper and hence often quite pricey.

P

PALETTE; wood, paper, metal or glass surface used to mix paints. Also term used to describe individual artists choice of colours.

PALETTE KNIFE; flexible painting tool that can be used for cleaning palette, mixing or applying IMPASTO paint.

PANEL; traditionally wood or metal slab for painting onto. Modern materials include MDF, plywood and hardboard. Look for purpose made and chamfered panels if possible. Hardboard [masonite] panels are fine if not too big and if supported by battens that prevent warping.

PAPER COLLÉ; A visual and tactile technique in which scraps of paper, with various textures are pasted to the picture surface to enrich or embellish areas. In addition to the actual texture of the paper, the print on tickets, newspapers, etc., can function as visual richness, or a decorative pattern in the same way as an artist's invented texture.

PATINA; 1. A natural film, usually greenish, that results from oxidation of bronze or other metallic material. 2. Colored pigments, chemicals, and so on, applied to a sculptural surface.

PASTEL; pigment bound in stick form like chalks. Can be oil pastels which are greasy and water resistant.

PERSPECTIVE; Any graphic system used to create the illusion of three-dimensional images and/or spatial relationships on a two-dimensional surface. There are several types of perspective: atmospheric, linear, and projection systems.

PHOTOGRAPHY; The art or practice of producing images of objects upon a photosensitive surface by the chemical action of light, discovered c. 1840.

PICTURE PLANE; The plane occupied by the physical surface of the picture. In most Representational painting, all the elements in the picture appear to recede from this plane, while trompe l'oeil effects are achieved by painting objects in such a way that they seem to project in front of the picture plane.

PIGMENT; original dry colouring matter from mineral, vegetable or animal origin in powder form. Differs from PAINT which is PIGMENT that has been dispersed in a binding agent such as OIL or ACRYLIC etc..

PLEIN AIR; A French term describing paintings done in the open air direct from the subject. Plein air painting became fashionable in the nineteenth century, and was central to the Impressionist movement.

POP ART; The name given to the form of art which uses, often satirically, the mundane products of mass popular culture, such as newspaper, magazine, television, and billboard advertising; comic strips and books; supermarket shelves, and so on, as its subject matter. It derived from certain early modern art forms and ideas, especially from Marcel Duchamps's ready-made and found objects of the 1920's through the 1950's. It began in England in the late 1950's and quickly spread to the United States in the 1960's.

PORTRAIT FORMAT; picture that is taller than wide. [see **LANDSCAPE FORMAT**]

POSITIVE (SHAPE, LINE, ETC.); The state in the artwork in which the art elements, or their combination, produce the subject. (See **NEGATIVE AREAS**)

POST-IMPRESSIONISM; The name applied to the style of a few artists at the end of the nineteenth century who sought to break away from the Impressionists and restore formal organization, decorative unity, and expressive meaning to art. The leaders in this movement were Paul Cézanne, Georges Seurat, Paul Gauguin, and Vincent van Gogh.

POSTMODERNISM; In the 1970's the dominant styles of art - Minimalism and Conceptualism - seemed to no longer fit in a world struggling with a myriad of social problems; as a result, a plurality of styles developed. Some Post-modernists forcefully expressed a desire to do away with art that seemed to have no meaningful content, and began to turn back to figurative art and the establishment of meaning. Other Post-modernists attempted to extend modern art in new ways by appropriating earlier styles, which they modified. Due to the sheer variety of sources and styles it is difficult to catergorize Post-modern artists with the same ease of earlier styles or movements.

PRIMARY COLOR; A fundamental color (red, blue, and yellow) that cannot be separated into any other colors. All other colors are produced from the mixing of primaries.

PRIMER, PRIMING; Priming a canvas, board, or other support simply means laying a ground. The paints specifically made for this purpose are sometimes called primers. The most commonly used today is acrylic gesso.

PRIMITIVE ART; The art of a people with a tribal social order or an early, though complex, stage of culture. The art of such people is often characterized by a heightened emphasis on form and content and a mysterious or vehement expressive content.

PRINT; any mark that has been made by transfer of image from one surface or form to another. Various methods have characteristics of process that make them unique. [see **GICLEE**, **LITHOGRAPH**, **ETCHING** etc..]

Q

R

REALISM, REALISM (ART MOVEMENT); A style of art that retains the basic impression of visual actuality without going to extremes of detail. In addition, realism attempts to relate and interpret the universal meanings that lie below the surface appearance. As a movement, Realism relates to painters like Honoré Daumier and Winslow Homer.

REFLECTED COLOR; Color on an object that bounces off adjacent objects.

REPRESENTATIONAL ART; A type of art in which the subject is presented through the visual elements so that the observer is reminded of actual objects. (See **NATURALISM** and **REALISM**).

REPRODUCTION; similar definition to PRINT but usually more mechanical involvement and denoting importance of accurate duplication of second image from first image. Often indicates that the picture is mass production.

ROMANTICISM; A movement of nineteenth-century artists such as Delacroix, Géricault, Turner, and others. It was the romantic spirit characterized by an experimental point of view and extolled spontaneity of expression, intuitive imagination, and the picturesque rather than a carefully organized, rational approach.

S

SATURATED COLOR; Pure intense color, unmixed with any black or white.

SCUMBLING; A technique used in all the opaque media including pastels. Scumbling involves dragging a dry, fairly thick layer of color in a deliberate uneven manner over a dried layer of another color, thus creating attractive broken color effects.

SECONDARY COLORS; The colors made by a mixture of two primary colors. Green, orange, and purple are all secondary colors.

SERIGRAPH; literally silkscreen print. The ink is squeezed onto the print surface through a mesh of silk or nylon gauze that has been prepared with blocked out areas. Printing process used for large scale printing i.e. posters, or fabric printing i.e. curtain material, or for special picture making processes that can be used without heavy duty presses. Favourite process for ORIGINAL PRINT production for many artists.

SGRAFFITO; A method whereby a layer of color is scratched into with a point to reveal either another layer of color below or the white of the ground, thus making a linear pattern.

SILK-SCREEN PRINT; see **SERIGRAPH**.

STRETCHER; expandable wooden frame that canvas is prepared onto before painting that enables the artist to adjust the tension of the surface.

SUCCESSIVE CONTRAST; The afterimage of a complementary color seen after viewing of color.

SUPPORT; Another word for the painting surface. A support can be anything, from paper to canvas or a wood panel.

SURREALISM; Influenced by Freudian psychology, this style of artistic expression emphasizes fantasy. Surrealist subjects are usually experiences revealed by the subconscious mind through the use of automatic techniques. Originally a literary movement and an outgrowth of Dadaism, Surrealism was established by a manifesto in 1924.

SYMBOL; The representation of a quality or situation through the use of another object, emblem, or sign. Examples are: the owl represents wisdom; the flag represents country - freedom - oppression; the color yellow represents cowardice.

SYMBOLISM; A movement that spread to painting in the 1880's. Paul Gauguin is considered to be the father of this movement. Symbolists tried to grapple with the notion of subjective ideas, stating that the senses are inseparable from human emotions and that people and objects are, therefore, merely symbols of a deeper existence beyond the everyday. It was not a style as such, and merely set a goal for artists to reach.

T

TEMPERA; Originally, all water-based paint, "tempered" with some form of gum was known as tempera, but the term is now used mainly for egg tempera, which was the main painting medium before the development of oils. Tempera is a tricky medium to use but can achieve beautiful effects, and after centuries of neglect it is now enjoying something of a revival.

TEMPERATURE; The relative warmth and coolness of hues or pigments.

TENEBRISM; A style of painting that exaggerates or emphasizes the effects of chiaroscuro. Large amounts of dark value are placed close to smaller areas of highly contrasting lights (and vice versa) in order to concentrate attention on important features.

TERTIARY COLORS; Mixtures of a primary and its adjacent secondary: for example, red-orange or blue-green; also called intermediate colors.

TINT; A light value of a color usually produced by the addition of white.

TONE; 1. The value or color character of a surface, determined by the quantity of light reflected from it. The amount of light reflected can be determined by the character of the medium that has been applied to the surface. 2. Color variety due to slight changes within the same hue.

TONKING; Removing surplus oil paint from the canvas by laying a sheet of absorbent paper over it, a correction method used when the surface has become too heavily loaded with paint to allow further work.

TRANSPARENT; Permitting light to penetrate and reflect off the white surface of the support or allowing another color to show through, as in a glaze.(The opposite of opaque)

TROMPE L'OEIL; A French phrase meaning "trick of the eye"; a technique that copies a subject with such exactitude that the viewer is tricked into believing he is seeing the subject in its natural form

U

V

W

WASH; A thin layer of paint covering a large area of of the support.

WATERCOLOUR; paint made by binding finely ground pigment in soluble gum. Traditional water-colours do not use white paint to lighten colour but instead rely on the transparency of the medium to reflect light through the paint film from the white paper below. [see **GOUACHE**]

WET-INTO-WET; Laying a new color before the previous one has dried. The effect in oils is not as dramatic as with water-colours but each new color is slightly modified by those below and adjacent, so that forms and colors merge into one another without hard boundaries.

WET-ON-DRY; Laying new (wet) color over a dried layer below.

WOOD BLOCK; engraving using hard wood block that has areas to be left blank carved away from surface to be inked.

WORKING DRAWING; A drawing made specifically as a basis for a painting, usually from earlier studies and/or photographs. Unlike a sketch, a working drawing establishes the entire composition, and is usually transferred to the painting surface.

X

XEROGRAPH; literally dry colour image. Process that uses dry colour "toner" which is melted onto paper with lasers. Highly technical process incorporating computer controlled machinery hence very high cost of equipment available through specialized studios catering for the advertising industry.

Y

Z

Special thanks to... **Man Creates ART Creates Man**....for permission to use some very useful definitions.